THE INTRUSIVE WORD

The Intrusive Word

Preaching to the Unbaptized

William H. Willimon

William B. Eerdmans Publishing Company
Grand Rapids, Michigan

Copyright © 1994 by Wm. B. Eerdmans Publishing Co.

255 Jefferson Ave. S.E., Grand Rapids, Michigan 49503

Printed in the United States of America

Library of Congress Cataloging-in-Publication Data

Willimon, William H.
The intrusive word: preaching to the unbaptized / William H. Willimon.
p.   cm.
Includes bibliographical references.
ISBN 0-8028-0706-2 (pbk.)
1. Preaching. 2. Evangelistic work. I. Title.
BV4211.2.W524 1994
251 — dc20   93-47548
CIP

To
Tom Long
who would have said it better

Contents

CONTENTS

Preface

In my last congregation, we decided that we needed to grow. We voted to launch a program of evangelism. Evangelism. You know what that means. It's the "We-had-better-go-out-and-get-new-members-or-we'll-die" syndrome. Beginning in the sixties, our church had begun a two-decade decline in membership, so we figured that a little church-growth strategy was in order.

We studied a program from our denomination telling us how to get new members. Among other things, the church-growth program advocated a system of door-to-door visitation. So we organized ourselves into groups of two and, on an appointed Sunday afternoon, we set out to visit, to invite people to our church.

The teams went out, armed with packets of pamphlets describing our congregation, pamphlets telling about our denomination, fliers portraying me, the smiling, accessible pastor, inviting people to our church. Each team was given a map with their assigned street.

Helen and Gladys were given a map. They were clearly told to go down Summit Drive and to *turn right*. That's what they were told. I heard the team leader tell them, "You go

1

down Summit Drive and turn right. Do you hear me, Helen, that's down Summit Drive and turn right?"

But Helen and Gladys, both approaching eighty, after lifetimes of teaching elementary school, were better at giving than receiving directions. They turned left, venturing down into the housing projects to the west of Summit Drive. We told them to turn right; they turned left.

Which meant that Helen and Gladys proceeded to evangelize the wrong neighborhood and thereby ran the risk of evangelizing the wrong people.

Late that afternoon, each team returned to the church to make their report. Helen and Gladys had only one interested person to report to us, a woman named Verleen. Nobody on their spurious route was interested in visiting our church, nobody but Verleen. She lived with her two children in a three-room apartment in the projects, we were told. Although she had never been to a church in her life, Verleen wanted to visit ours.

This is what you get, I said to myself, when you don't follow directions, when you won't do what the pastor tells you to do. This is what you get, a woman from the projects named Verleen.

The next Sunday, Helen and Gladys proudly presented Verleen at the eleven o'clock service, along with her two feral-looking children. Verleen liked the service so much she said that she wanted to attend the Women's Thursday Morning Bible Study. Helen and Gladys said they would pick her up on Thursday.

On Thursday, Verleen appeared, proudly clutching her new Bible, a gift of Helen's circle, the first Bible Verleen had ever seen, much less owned.

I was leading the study that morning, a study on the lection for the coming Sunday, Luke 4, the story of Jesus' temptation in the wilderness. "Have any of you ever been faced with temptation and, with Jesus' help, resisted?" I asked the group

2

after presenting my material. "Have any of you refused some temptation because of your Christian commitment?"

One of the women told about how, just the week before, there was some confusion in the supermarket checkout line, and before she knew it, she was standing in the supermarket parking lot with a loaf of bread that she hadn't paid for.

"At first I thought," she confessed, "why should I pay for it? They have enough money here as it is. But then I thought, 'No, you are a Christian.' So I went back in the store and paid them for that loaf of bread."

I made some approving comment.

It was then that Verleen spoke. "A couple of years ago, I was into cocaine really big. You know what that's like! You know how that stuff makes you crazy. Well, anyway, my boyfriend, not the one I've got now, the one who was the daddy of my first child, that one, well, we knocked over a gas station one night — got two hundred dollars out of it. It was as simple as taking candy from a baby. Well, my boyfriend, he says to me, 'Let's knock off that Seven-eleven down on the corner.' And something in me, it says, 'No, I've held up that gas station with you, but I ain't going to hold up no convenience store.' He beat the hell out of me, but I still said No. It felt great to say No, 'cause that's the only time in my life I ever said No to anything. Made me feel like I was somebody."

Through the stunned silence I managed to mutter, "Well, er, uh, that's resisting temptation. That's sort of what this text is about. And now it's time for our closing prayer."

After I stumbled out of the church parlor and was standing out in the parking lot, helping Helen into her Plymouth, she said to me, "You know, I can't wait to get home and get on the phone and invite people to come next Thursday! Your Bible studies used to be dull. I think I can get a good crowd for this!"[1]

1. Adapted from my "Last Word," in *The Christian Ministry,* May-June 1993.

*   *   *

I ought to dedicate this book to Verleen. I dedicated my *Peculiar Speech: Preaching to the Baptized* to Walter Brueggemann because he kindled my thinking about the peculiarity of Christian preaching. Walt knows more about the Bible than either Verleen or I. But maybe Verleen knows more about evangelism than either of us preachers. At least she taught me a great deal about evangelism that morning at the Bible study.

That is, Verleen taught me that evangelism is not about getting new members for the church, though a new church is evangelism's harvest. Evangelism is not about helping more nice, buttoned-down, middle-class folk like me or Walt to find deeper meaning in our lives. Evangelism is a gracious, unmanageable, messy by-product of the intrusions of God.

Verleen was not the only one who intruded into our nice, bourgeois club called Northside United Methodist Church. She had been brought there, I believe, by Another. Time and again in our life together as the church, just when we get everything all figured out, the pews all bolted down, and everyone blissfully adjusted to the status quo, God has intruded, inserting some topsy-turvy-turned life like Verleen just to remind the baptized that God is large, unmanageable, and full of surprises.

This book asserts to the baptized that preaching in the service of anything less than a living, intrusive God is not worth the effort. As Barth told us, "The church is not a tool to uphold the world or to further its progress. It is not an instrument to serve either what is old or what is new. The church and preaching are not ambulances on the battlefield of life. . . . [T]he moment preaching makes these things its end, it becomes superfluous."[2]

2. Karl Barth, *Homiletics,* trans. G. W. Bromiley and Donald E. Daniels (Louisville: Westminster/John Knox Press, 1991), pp. 63-64.

Superfluity is a big problem for my church family, mainline Protestantism. At best we are little more than "ambulances on the battlefield of life." At worst we are a rather sanctimonious self-help society, a Rotary club, meeting on Sundays at eleven. Evangelism, to the biblical preacher, "in large part consists of attending to and participating in the transformational drama that is enacted in the biblical text itself."[3] That's the purpose of the sermons that follow the chapters — to demonstrate one preacher's efforts to expose a congregation to the imaginative models of reality that are made available in preaching from the Bible and to invite them to participate in those models. Evangelistic preaching is, in Walter Brueggemann's words, "doing the text again."[4]

I contend that, through evangelism, through repeated confrontation with the intrusive grace of God, the church can be born again. By letting God use us in God's never-ending pursuit of the unbaptized, the baptized can rediscover what it means for us to be the church, that unlikely gathering of those who are called to sign, signal, and witness to the graciousness of God in a world dying for lack of salvation.

Peculiar Speech pondered the implications of speaking, week after week, to the baptized, the already-evangelized or still-being-evangelized crowd who gather on Sundays at your church. Now I want to consider what it means to preach to the unbaptized, to those baptized or unbaptized who have not yet heard the gospel in its life-changing, disruptive fullness. Evangelism is a matter of addressing those who live by narratives other than the gospel, and those people are usually outsiders but sometimes insiders. The good news of Jesus is so odd that we never get so good at hearing it and living on the basis of it that we don't need to hear it again.

3. The definition is Walter Brueggemann's in his *Biblical Perspectives on Evangelism* (Nashville: Abingdon Press, 1993), p. 8.

4. Brueggemann, p. 8.

I don't mean thereby to imply that preaching is everything in evangelism. Preaching, the articulation of the Word in the words of a sermon, is only one aspect of the church's evangelistic commotion. William Abraham defines evangelism as "that set of intentional activities which is governed by the goal of initiating people into the kingdom of God for the first time."[5] (What's so special about "the first time"? Our first brush with the kingdom of God is about as important as our first kiss.) *The Intrusive Word* contends that the baptized never get over evangelism, that the attempt to evangelize others enables us continually to be evangelized. The best part about Abraham's thought on this issue is that, although he emphasizes the first steps in the faith, in very Wesleyan fashion, Abraham stresses evangelism as a long process, rarely if ever accomplished in a moment, always much more than words can say. When American evangelicalism made conversion a radically individualized affair, conversion was "uprooted from that social and ecclesial context, making it an orphan, hopelessly starved of moral and theological content."[6] Evangelism is a church (i.e., political, corporate, communal, sacramental) process. Nobody gets converted to *Christianity* in a vacuum. Every true conversion takes place in a socio-historical context. And it takes time.

Abraham notes that evangelism changes not only the convert but also the context. That is my point. Even as Verleen was converted, so Verleen's conversion converted the church (and its pastor!). While I am all in favor of changing the world, right now I would most like to change the church. One of the most gracious by-products of evangelistic preaching is the potential conversion of the church, the transformation of God's people from an enclave of the culturally content into a beachhead for divine invasion. Easter. God

5. William J. Abraham, *The Logic of Evangelism* (Grand Rapids: Eerdmans, 1989), p. 95.
6. Abraham, p. 123.

bless you, Verleen, for allowing us to catch a glimpse of how our baptism means more than even we knew.

Duke University Chapel   William H. Willimon
Pentecost, 1993

Take Away the Stone
John August Swanson, 1993; watercolor on paper, 18″ x 12″

8

"Lord of Life"

Fifth Sunday in Lent
John 11:1-16, 17-44

"I am the resurrection and the life. Those who believe in me, even though they die, shall live."

John 11:25

Marcus Aurelius, in his Stoic Code, says that the wise person is the one who has ceased "to be whirled around" by external determination. Wisdom arises in that moment, at the end of that educational process whereby you take possession of your life and your strings cease to be pulled by someone or something other.

In my freshman seminar, we talk about freedom. I ask the students, "Are you free?" And they always say they are.

"I was fortunate," they say; "my parents always gave me lots of freedom, trusted me to make wise decisions. I am free."

Then I inquire, "Would you have been free not to come to Duke? What would they have said if, upon completing high school, you had declared, 'I wish to spend my life working on Chevrolets'? Would you have been free to do so?"

And bold assertions of freshman freedom wilt. And we realize how much of our lives has been determined, determined so skillfully and subtly that we are unaware when our strings are being pulled. We are not so much "free" as we are happy slaves. Hobbes described our claims of freedom as a mere phantasm of consciousness: "If a wooden top, lashed by the boys . . . sometimes spinning, sometimes hitting men on the shins were sensible of its own motion [it] would think that it proceeded from its own will." A spinning top thinks it's free, just because it's spinning. Similarly, Spinoza cynically said that if a stone could think, when thrown across a river, that stone "would believe itself to be completely free and would think that it continued in motion solely because of its own wish."*

Free? Who pulls your strings?

*   *   *

Once the biggest, most overly built building on campus was this chapel. Now it's the hospital. What does that tell you? I should say the biggest, most overly built, least effective building is the hospital. One reason why it's so big is that it serves as our biggest hedge against our greatest fear — namely, death. And while Duke Hospital hasn't yet found a cure for our dying, we believe it to be the best cure we have, so we put a great deal of resources into the effort.

Health care is one thing; dealing with death is a much greater thing, requiring the largest, most expensive building on campus. I'm saying that something more than "health care" is pulling our strings.

Ford Motor Company spends more on employee health care each year than on steel. The whole world has become a hospital.

*Cited in Irvin D. Yalom, *Existential Psychotherapy* (New York: Basic Books, 1980), p. 289.

I'm saying that *death* is pulling our strings. We may tame the national deficit, but even Hillary's health care plan won't solve death. And if we can't do something with our dying, we haven't done much with anything. We are jerked around by death.

The pharaohs had their pyramids. We had our arms race with the Russians. Now we've got our national health care. We build bombs and we build hospitals for much the same reason. Anytime we humans get together to do something about the world, the main agenda, the only project we undertake, that toward which most of our resources are flowing, is death. We are jerked around by death.

*   *   *

Lazarus was ill over in Bethany, being cared for by his sisters, Mary and Martha (John 12:1-8). You remember Mary, the impractical one who "wasted" that expensive perfume, pouring it all over Jesus when he last visited the sisters. Remember Martha, the practical one who made her own matzo from scratch and was good in the kitchen (Luke 10:38-42). The sisters sent a message to Jesus: "Lord, Lazarus, whom you love, is ill" (John 11:3).

Watch Jesus. He brushes off the message, saying something like "*This* illness doesn't lead to death." (A strange statement, since Jesus, not having seen Lazarus, doesn't know what his illness is.)

Curiously, after receiving the sisters' anguished summons to Lazarus's sickbed, Jesus hangs around *two more days* before heading off to Bethany. Explain that, would you. Jesus, Mr. Compassion, is summoned to the bedside of a friend near death. You'd think he'd drop everything and take the night train to Bethany. It's not that he's in the middle of something important. John just says that Jesus "stayed two days longer in the place where he was" (v. 6).

11

When Jesus finally gets around to heading off to Bethany, his disciples warn him: "Your enemies are out there, just waiting to kill you, and you're going there again?" (v. 8). Jesus pays them, and their talk about deadly opposition, no mind.

"Well," Thomas says, "let's go with him so that we can all hang together" (v. 16). Death is everywhere. Lazarus is dying; the disciples are resigned to their dying. Yet Jesus seems curiously oblivious to the dying, somehow free.

When Jesus finally gets to Bethany a couple of days later, it's all over. Lazarus has been wrapped in his shroud, entombed for four days. Martha comes out to meet Jesus, and she gives him a piece of her mind.

"Lord, if you had gotten off your ——— and been here, my brother wouldn't be dead" (v. 21).

Jesus says, "Your brother will rise again."

Martha says, "Yeah, yeah, I know all that stuff about the resurrection of the dead on the last day, someday." What Martha wants is not some pious talk like "He's gone to a better place" or "Martha, this is God's will." She wants her brother back. An unmarried woman, in that day, in that patriarchal world, what's going to become of her and her sister, alone, vulnerable? Without Lazarus, she's as good as dead.

But Jesus isn't talking abstract theology of the resurrection. He doesn't say to her, "Believe that *someday* Lazarus will be resurrected" or "You'll see him again in heaven." Jesus says, "*I am* the resurrection. *I am* life" (v. 25). Not "I have come to discuss the idea of resurrection."

"I am resurrection." "I am life."

Do you believe it? And old practical, pots-and-pans, straight-talking Martha makes the most extravagant, effusive, explicit statement of faith in the gospel up to this time: "Yes, Lord, I believe that you are the Messiah, the Son of God, the one coming into the world" (v. 27).

And they go out to the cemetery where everyone is weeping. John says that Jesus was now "greatly disturbed in spirit and deeply moved," and when he saw the tomb where Lazarus was, "Jesus began to weep" (vv. 33, 35). Jesus, Mr. Resurrection, Mr. Life, just hates death.

"Take away the stone," orders Jesus. Good old, practical, realistic Martha says, "Lord, already there is a stench because he has been dead for four days" (v. 39).

But with a voice loud enough to wake the dead, Jesus shouts, "Lazarus, come out!" (v. 43). And the dead man comes out, "his hands and feet bound with strips of cloth, and his face wrapped in a cloth" (v. 44). All tied up, bound by death, like a mummy, there stands Lazarus.

Jesus commands, "Unbind him, and let him go."

$$*\qquad*\qquad*$$

With whom do you identify in this wonderfully weird, realistic story? Martha? Mary? Yes, there is much grief in this life. We're always having funerals. Or perhaps Lazarus is us, because there is much death in this life, much binding, mummified caughtness and death. And Jesus just hates death. He will not be jerked around by death, will not let dying or fear of it control his calendar. At the cemetery his words are "Take away the stone!" and "Lazarus, come out!" and "Unbind him, let him go!" And we wonder if he is calling to us, shouting loud enough to wake the dead.

Lazarus comes forth from the tomb. In two weeks, Jesus shall enter the tomb. The powers of death — the folk at the Pentagon, the religious establishment, the fickle crowd, the guardians of the status quo — will at last have their way with Jesus. The raising of Lazarus is a kind of preview, a glimpse of Easter, an opening skirmish between death and life. When Lazarus strides forth from the tomb, it provokes fierce hostility from Jesus' critics. If you don't know why, then you don't

13

know much about how the powers of death hold on tight to their grip over our lives, the ways in which the way of death wants to pull our strings, make us pay.

The whole world is a graveyard, and death is omnivorous. In the face of death, we, like the disciples, adjust. Jesus weeps (v. 35). We adapt; Jesus is "greatly disturbed" (vv. 33, 38). Jesus just hates death. Maybe the only illness that leads to death (v. 3) is the illness of adjustment, adaptation to death. Once Lazarus is raised, the deadly powers-that-be move into action, and the serpent's egg plot to kill Jesus is hatched. And yet, Jesus is free.

What would it take for *you* to be free?

Earlier, Jesus had said (in a loud voice, I think), "I came that they may have life, and have it abundantly" (10:10); "I give them eternal life, and they will never perish. No one will snatch them out of my hand" (10:28).

So go ahead, try to adjust yourself to the death, the deadness. But take care. The Lord of Life has warned, "The hour is coming when all who are in their graves will hear his voice and will come out" (5:28-29).

And if the Lord of Life makes you free, you'll be free indeed.

1

The Miracle of Hearing

When I emerged from seminary and began to preach, I thought that about the worst fate that could befall me as a preacher was not to be heard. It was my task, through the homiletical, rhetorical arts, to bridge the gap, the great communicative gap between speaker and listener. I now know that I had been taught to misconstrue the gap. The gap, the evangelical distance that ought to concern the preacher, is not one of time, the time between Jesus and us, nor is it one of communication, the space between speaker and listener. The gap that is the main concern of the evangelical preacher is the space between us and the gospel. Theology, rather than style, rhetoric, or method, is our concern.

There are many reasons why we fail to communicate as preachers that have to do with our limitations as preachers. We don't communicate because we lack certain homiletical skills, because we don't prepare, because we don't know enough about the gospel, because we misunderstand the human condition. But there are also many excellent reasons for our failure to communicate.

In sermon preparation, I quickly learned that some of my

most unfaithful preaching arose in that moment when, after having studied the biblical text, I asked myself, "So what?"

That's where the trouble starts, in my homiletical attempt to answer the "So what?" question. Trouble is, I will invariably misconstrue the communicative gap between my people and the gospel. My answer to the "So what?" question will be limited by my present horizons, by conventional ideas of what can and cannot be. Evangelism, unlike apologetics, seeks transformation on the part of speaker and hearer.[1] Evangelism expects and promises transformation. Refusing to traffic in the conventional epistemologies of the present age and its beneficiaries, evangelism says that we will never know anything worth knowing without conversion.

> Put away your former way of life, your old self, corrupt and deluded by its lusts, and . . . be renewed in the spirit of your minds, and . . . clothe yourselves with the new self, created according to the likeness of God in true righteousness and holiness.
>
> Ephesians 4:22-24

The images of stripping off clothes and throwing away our past are surely baptismal. Everything starts and ends with baptism. If our speech doesn't move uninformed people outside the church toward baptism, or at least move jaded, tired, cynical people inside the church to a renewal of their baptism, our talk is not evangelical. Apologetics is what we do when we don't want to risk being transformed. Apologetics is Josh McDowell coming to campus to talk about sex, and then, in the last five minutes of his speech, dangling out

---

1. See Stanley Hauerwas's criticism of apologetics in William H. Willimon and Stanley M. Hauerwas, *Preaching to Strangers: Evangelism in Today's World* (Louisville: Westminster/John Knox Press, 1992), pp. 1-15.

Jesus as the answer to everything that ails us, including our sick sex. All that proves is that sex is more important than Jesus because we start with sex, bowing to its dominance in our lives, and then, after having established an intellectual community on that basis, slyly move our hearers to think about Jesus. Apologetics gives up too much intellectual territory before the battle begins.

That's what I loved about what Verleen reminded us of in our church. She could not have been helped by mere agreement. Anything less than transformation, conversion, would have been too little for Verleen. We Christian communicators have expected too little from the gospel.

This is my major disagreement with Leander Keck's *The Church Confident*.[2] Realizing that mainline Protestant Christianity is in big trouble, Keck calls upon us Protestant preachers to be more confident in what we have to say, to assert, ever more skillfully and confidently, pretty much what we have said before. Keck's is a justification, albeit a very skillfully done justification, for business as usual in the American church. The faith that he would have us assert more confidently is the pre-1940s faith that Americans (if church numbers are to be believed) appear to have relinquished. The mainline Protestantism that Keck defends fared quite well during times of American cultural confidence; after all, it was the faith engendered by that culture, the faith of mainline Protestant liberalism, which so hoped to be of service to the

2. Leander E. Keck, *The Church Confident* (Nashville: Abingdon Press, 1993). Keck dismisses my book (with Stanley Hauerwas) *Resident Aliens: Life in the Christian Colony* (Nashville: Abingdon Press, 1989) as "inappropriate for the mainline churches" (Keck, p. 76). In this book, I continue to bet that Keck is wrong in his belief that the mainline churches are "tone deaf to such a summons" (Keck, p. 75). In this respect, I am more confident about mainline American Protestantism than Keck. I really do believe that we are capable of being so faithful (rather than so confident in the theology and style of our recent past) that Americans might again find us Christians to be interesting.

culture. However, as the seventies began and increasing numbers of Americans realized that something was wrong in their nation, in their marriages, and in their families, the self-confident liberalism of the mainliners wilted, and people either deserted us in droves or greeted us with a yawn. I see no reason to urge more confidence in preaching *that* tired message.

Besides, there are excellent reasons why we don't communicate. People bring many things with them in their listening to a sermon. Having been preconditioned, their ears are not in tune with the message; their understanding is blocked by metaphors that enable them to participate in the culture but that make it difficult for them to hear the gospel. We evangelists ought to throw the mantle of forgiveness over some of our homiletical failures. Desiring too desperately to communicate, at any cost, can lead us into apostasy. The odd way in which God has saved us presents a never-ending challenge to those who are called to talk about it.

Recently, a woman who was a practitioner of something she called "destructivist art" came to my class. Destructivist art involves, at least in her case, throwing hydrochloric acid on a canvas, while viewers watch the canvas rot due to the eating away of the canvas by the acid. This is alleged to be some sort of statement about our cultural situation.

After she showed the class examples of her art, some of the class said, "This is the most wonderful thing we've ever seen."

However, the majority of the class felt totally excluded by her communication. Many of them were even angry. "This is not art!" they blurted out. "This is demeaning to the whole notion of art. If this is art, anybody can do it."

She responded, "Anyone could do it, but the important thing is that *I* did it. The other important thing is that you don't know what I am doing."

She responded to their questions with grace, good humor, and sensitivity. However, by the end of the class, most of the students were still unconvinced, uncomprehending of her work.

The thing that impressed me as a Christian communicator was her absolute willingness to have them not understand her. She seemed utterly willing for them to walk out of the class, as befuddled by her art at the end of the class as they were when the class began.

"There are good reasons for not understanding this art. Don't be so hard on yourself," she reassured them. "This art is very demanding on the viewer. If I am really making a critique of the present structures of society, then if one is caught in one of those structures, or benefitting from those structures, there are good reasons why one should not be able to understand this art. In a way, your inability to comprehend this art is, in itself, a validation of what I'm claiming to be the aims of this art."

The session with the artist left me with this question: Can we preachers respect the gospel enough to allow people not to understand it? We are not responsible for all failures of communication. The gospel itself, in collision with the corruptions engendered by life in a democratic, capitalist society, bears some of the responsibility for people not hearing.

We preachers so want to be heard that we are willing to make the gospel more accessible than it really is, to remove the scandal, the offense of the cross, to deceive people into thinking that it is possible to hear without conversion. This is the great lie behind most of my apologetics, the deceit that it is possible to hear the gospel while we are still trapped in outmoded or culturally conditioned patterns of thought and hearing. How are we extricated from such patterns? Only by being confronted by the gospel. How does the gospel manage to work such power among epistemologically enslaved folk like us? I don't know. It's a miracle.

19

The Listener as King

In this respect we are heirs of Charles G. Finney, a lawyer called by God from his law practice in 1821 by "a retainer from the Lord Jesus Christ to plead his cause." Finney invented the "protracted meeting" for revivals, introduced the "anxious bench" for sinners, and developed the team approach to planning for a revival. "Revival is not a miracle, or dependent on a miracle in any sense. It is a purely philosophical [i.e. scientific] result of the right use of the constituted means," said Finney in his 1835 *Lectures on Revivalism*. Today, we have forgotten that there was once a time when evangelists were forced to defend their "new measures" for revivals, that there was once a time when preachers had to defend their preoccupation with listener response to their Calvinist detractors who thought that the gospel was more important than its listeners.

I am here arguing that revivals *are* miraculous, that the gospel is so odd, so against the grain of our natural inclinations and the infatuations of our culture, that nothing less than a miracle is required in order for there to be true hearing. My position is therefore closer to that of the Calvinist Jonathan Edwards than to the position of Finney. Edwards labored as pastor in Northampton, Massachusetts, for an uneventful seven lean years until his congregation experienced a series of what Edwards called "surprising conversions." Edwards, one of the greatest minds America has produced, was wonderfully befuddled by this outbreak of religious vitality. In 1737 he wrote an account of the affair, delightfully called *A Faithful Narrative of the Surprising Work of God in the Conversion of Many Hundred Souls in Northampton, and Neighboring Towns and Villages*. I like to think that Edwards was such a great mind, had such an understanding of the peculiarity of the gospel, coupled with an awareness of the intransigence of his people, that he was therefore genuinely surprised when anyone heard, really heard and responded to his preaching. We ought also to be surprised.

The homiletical future, alas, lay with Finney rather than Edwards. The logical culmination of Finney's theological weaknesses, the "new measures" for our day, are to be found not only in the inductive preaching proponents who measure all preaching on the basis of listener response but also in the new genre of church-marketing books typified by the work of George Barna, church-growth strategist. In popular books for clergy with titles like *Marketing the Church* and *User Friendly Churches,* Barna tells us that

> Jesus Christ was a communications specialist. He communicated His message in diverse ways, and with results that would be a credit to modern advertising and marketing agencies. Notice the Lord's approach: He identified His target audience, determined their need, and delivered His message directly. . . . He promoted His product in the most efficient way possible: by communicating with the 'hot prospects.'
>
> Don't underestimate the marketing lessons Jesus taught. He understood His product thoroughly, developed an unparalleled distribution system, advanced a method of promotion that has penetrated every continent, and offered His product at a price that is within the grasp of every consumer (without making the product so accessible that it lost its value).[3]

3. George Barna, *Marketing the Church: What They Never Taught You about Church Growth* (Colorado Springs: NavPress, 1988), p. 50. For an extensive, evangelical critique of Barna and the entire church-marketing movement, see Douglas D. Webster, *Selling Jesus* (Downers Grove, IL: InterVarsity Press, 1992). Walter Brueggemann's corrective on Barna's type of "church growth" is helpful here:

  evangelism is related *to church growth,* related but in no way synonymous. In speaking of evangelism, one must speak of church growth, but only

In *Resident Aliens: Life in the Christian Colony,* Stanley Hauerwas and I suggested that there is much atheism lurking behind some of our preaching, pastoral care, and church administration. Atheism is the conviction that the presence and power of God are unessential to the work of ministry, that we can find the right technique, the proper approach, and the appropriate attitude and therefore will not need God to validate our ministry. If Jesus was the "communications specialist" that Barna claims him to be, why in the world did he waste so much time teaching "in parables," which very few understood? Above all, if he was so good at communication, why on earth was he crucified?

We must learn to preach again in such a way as to demonstrate that, if there is no Holy Spirit, if Jesus has not been raised from the dead, then our preaching is doomed to fall upon deaf ears. Our preaching ought to be so confrontive, so in violation of all that contemporary Americans think they know, that it requires no less than a miracle to be heard. We preach best with a reckless confidence in the power of the gospel to evoke the audience it deserves.

I find myself agreeing with Robin R. Meyers when he says, "Preachers are too eager to make sure that everyone understands, that everyone gets it. This inevitably means that too

---

at the end of the dramatic process, and not any sooner. Evangelism is never aimed at institutional enhancement or aggrandizement. It is aimed simply and solely at summoning people to new, liberated obedience to the true governor of all created reality. The church is a modest gathering locus for those serious about the new governance. There must be such a gathering, . . . because the new governance is inherently against autonomy, isolation, and individualism. The church grows because more and more persons change allegiance, switch worlds, accept the new governance and agree to the unending and difficult task of appropriating the news in practical ways. "Church growth" misserves evangelism, however, when the church is allied with consumerism, for then the church talks people out of the very obedience to which the news summons us. (*Biblical Perspectives on Evangelism* [Nashville: Abingdon Press, 1993], p. 45)

much of the obvious is explained, and too little of the mysterious is described."

Yet I part company with Meyers when he contends that "We are not using symbolic language to achieve some sort of conceptual precision, rather we are using metaphors to generate the insight that comes from recognizing common human experience."[4] "Common human experience" doesn't exist, and even if it did, it should not be confused with the gospel. There are only different stories that evoke and engender various kinds of human experiences. The gospel is one such story, a story that we believe to be not only mysterious and interesting but also *true*. Church is the human experience evoked by the gospel. Preaching is not a means to evoke certain "common human experience" through the artful use of metaphor and simile. Preaching means to engender experience we would never have had without the gospel.

In Meyers's book *Ears to Hear,* he speaks about preaching as if our challenge were mainly a problem of our inadequate use of rhetoric, a problem of style, delivery, method. His book is rather typical of the tendency within modern homiletics to fixate on communicative method rather than theological substance, a tendency that I pilloried in *Peculiar Speech.*[5]

---

4. Robin R. Meyers, *With Ears to Hear: Preaching As Self-Persuasion* (Cleveland: Pilgrim Press, 1993), p. 79. The problem with Meyers's book is not simply its over-reliance on Fred B. Craddock's *As One without Authority* (Enid, OK: Phillips University Press, 1971), but its rather shocking thesis that "Self-persuasion theory rests on one very simple but central premise: the messages we generate for ourselves are more authoritative than those from an outside source. This clear and decisive break with classical rhetoric locates persuasion at the ear of the listener, not at the mouth of the rhetor. And there exists a substantial body of research to back up the claim that when it comes to authority, the holiest of trinities is Me, Myself, and I" (Meyers, p. 49). As a wonderful statement of the uphill battle to be waged each Sunday by the evangelical preacher, I can do no better than this. As a basis for homiletical theory, such a thesis must be rejected on the basis of the peculiarity of trinitarian faith.

5. *Peculiar Speech* (Grand Rapids: Eerdmans, 1992), pp. 49-53.

There is certainly much to be learned by preachers about rhetoric and method, and Meyers's book is helpful. However, I am arguing that failure to hear is also based upon the nature of the gospel. When Kierkegaard observed, "Truth is not nimble on its feet . . . it is not its own evangelist," perhaps he was indicating how large a task we have in communicating the gospel in a culture of lies. Where we want the gospel to be gracious it is judgmental, and where we want it to be judgment it is all grace. The gospel itself shares some of the "blame" for our communicative failures, contending, as the gospel does, that the solution to what ails us lies somewhere out beyond our selves.

G. K. Chesterton once said that, if you are trying to communicate something to another person and the person says, "I don't understand," you will reach for some metaphor. You will say, "Well, it's like. . . ." Then, if the person still responds, "I don't understand," you will try another metaphor. If the person still does not understand, then you must say, "You don't understand."

More than that, I am arguing that bad preaching, as Meyers describes it — preaching so anxious that "everyone gets it" that it ends up expecting too much and saying too little — is often a factor of bad theology. We have so little trust in the power of the gospel, through the enablement of the Holy Spirit, to evoke the listeners that the gospel deserves, that we either simplify, simplify, reducing the gospel to a slogan for a bumper sticker, or else we poetically describe, describe, obfuscating the gospel with some allegedly "common human experience" that is not the gospel. People live in the grip of stories that are not the gospel, stories that cannot generate the life for which they deeply yearn. Therefore I agree with Walter Brueggemann when he says that "evangelism means inviting people into these stories [the gospel] as the definitional story of our life, and thereby authorizing people to give up, abandon, and renounce other stories that have shaped their lives in false or distorting ways."[6]

Easter as the Basis for Christian Preaching

The gospel is an intrusion among us, not something arising out of us. Easter is the ultimate intrusion of God. The gap between our alliances with death and the God of life as revealed on Easter is the ultimate gap with which gospel preaching must contend. Easter is an embarrassment the church can't get around. Yet in this embarrassment is the engine that drives our preaching. It is only because Jesus has been raised from the dead that I have confidence in preaching. It is only on the basis of the risen Christ's return to his disheartened followers after Easter that I presume that he has made me an agent of gospel subversion through preaching. If God did not triumph over Caesar and all the legions of death on Easter, then God will never triumph on Sunday in my church over *The Wall Street Journal* and Leo Buscaglia.

I don't preach Jesus' story in the light of my experience, as some sort of helpful symbol or myth that is usefully illumined by my story.[7] Rather, I am invited by Easter to interpret my story in the light of God's triumph in the resurrection. Only because we worship a resurrected Lord can we risk preaching. Our claims for preaching have little to do with a savvy utilization of various contemporary rhetorical insights; rather, our claims arise from our very peculiar convictions about a very particular God. The essential patience required of preachers,

6. Brueggemann, p. 10.
7. I fear this is what David Buttrick comes close to in *Homiletic* (Philadelphia: Fortress Press, 1987), pp. 399-404, in his description of preaching Mark 16:1-8 as "symbol." Yet Buttrick's discussion of the resurrection and preaching (pp. 450-51) certainly seems to confirm what I am claiming about preaching's linkage to Easter.

freedom from homiletical anxiety over the reaction of our listeners, is possible only if in fact Jesus did rise from the tomb.

As Rowan Williams says,

> the Christian proclamation of the resurrection of the crucified just man, his return to his unfaithful friends and his empowering of them to forgive in his name offers a paradigm of the "saving" process; yet not only a paradigm. It is a story which is itself an indispensable agent in the completion of this process, because it witnesses to the one personal agent in whose presence we may have full courage to "own" ourselves as sinners and full hope for a humanity whose identity is grounded in a recognition and affirmation by nothing less than God. It is a story which makes possible the comprehensive act of *trust*.[8]

I wish that I might preach in such a way as to require a miracle, a resurrection, in order to be heard. I wish that I might preach in such a way as to demonstrate my outrageous trust in the continuing reality of Easter, my utter dependence on God's inclination to work the unexpected. So many of the Easter narratives end with the command "Go, tell." We may go and tell, not only because we now have, after Easter, some news to tell — namely, that Jesus shall reign — but also because, after Easter, we have the means to tell, principally because the risen Christ continues to work life out of death in us wherever this story is faithfully told. God comes to us, comes back to us.

Does the sermon that follows embody, at least in a limited way, Williams's assertion that the story of Easter is itself "an indispensable agent" in the completion of Easter in today's church?

8. Rowan Williams, *Resurrection* (London: Darton, Longman & Todd, 1982), p. 49.

"God Came Back"

Easter Sunday
Jeremiah 31:1-6; Matthew 28:1-9

"The Lord appeared. . . . I have loved you with an everlasting love; therefore I have continued my faithfulness to you. . . . Again you shall take your tambourines, and go forth in the dance of the merrymakers."

Jeremiah 31:3-4

G od did with dead Jesus what God wants to do to us every day.

This is the thick theological thought I'd like to emulsify in your brain this morning.

Nobody expected Easter. Nothing in this life prepared us for what was encountered out at the cemetery that morning. Those who went to the empty tomb that morning were unprepared, unbelieving of what they saw. They had never, could never in their wildest imaginations conceive of resurrection, life over death. Was that the problem with those astounded women?

Only partly. We had hints, long before Easter, that God was in the business of life, not death. But we, too much in the business of death, cannot always believe life. That's the problem.

It is the church's claim, in reading Old and New Testaments together, that *the whole saving history of God's dealing with us is a story of the steady overcoming of death's dominion.* The resurrection of Jesus is the final signal, not the opening shot, of God's ultimate victory over *Thanatos,* that death has at last been crushed. Why, just a couple of Sundays past we watched Jesus raise old, dead Lazarus with a shout. That resuscitation, along with Jesus' myriad of signs, signals, and cures, ought to be seen as a series of Easter preludes, small resurrections, restorations to life. Jesus' birth is a sign that death is terminal. In every episode of Jesus' life, death is losing its grip. Every time somebody once crippled stands up and walks, or blind eyes see, or prisoners break free, death is being dispelled in Jesus, and life is having its way over mortality and its allies. By the time we get to Easter, asks Aidan Kavanaugh, how could the tomb be anything but empty?

I'll tell you why the women who peered into the dark tomb were shocked. There's something about us — despite centuries of death's death and divine assaults on morbidity — that still finds comfort in the darkness of a tomb, the vampire's deadly kiss, the friendly confines of predictability, habit, thanatotic routine. When I travel, I always — after I check into my motel — lay out my toothbrush, toothpaste, hairbrush, just as they are fixed at home. I hate surprises.

And who among us does not relish snuggling under the covers on a cold night, gleefully on our way to narcosis? And who here loves to be awakened in the morning, once again shocked that day has come, life has resumed, and we are yet alive? We love our deaths, our duties, our well-shouldered drudgeries, limits, rules, and habits. Finitude fits us like a glove.

When our beloved Amy, Duke freshman, faithful member of our Chapel Choir, was crushed by a bus last fall, a therapist from CAPS (Counseling and Psychological Services) appeared and told a group of grieving students, "You're all doing just

28

fine, right on schedule with your grief, this is good." Therapy as *Thanatos*.

But five days later, at Amy's memorial service, the Chapel Choir (never ones to respect authority) stood and sang defiantly, raucously, "For as in Adam all die, even so in Christ shall all be made alive!" And God came back. Death slinked off campus, his great victory party ruined by a choir that refused to defer to death.

"There arose a Pharaoh in Egypt who did not know Joseph," says Exodus 1:8. That Pharaoh made the Hebrew children slaves, placed upon their backs unbearable burdens, and killed their boy babies (first of many genocides against God's chosen).

Are you surprised that lots of us loved it in slavery? Oh, the work was hard, but at least we got three square meals a day. Pharaoh's slavery is not so bad once you learn to adjust. The bent back grows calloused to the sting of the master's whip. Adapt. Adjust.

But God came back.

To Moses, minding his own business, a bush burst into flame. A voice. "I've heard the cry of my people. I'm going to free them, go head-to-head with Pharaoh, and guess who's going to help me?"

Moses stammered. But —

God came back.

Israel, once free, was not free long. From the north came chariots, warhorses, iron spears of the Assyrians. Cities burned and pillaged. Whole Hebrew tribes carted off into cruel exile (first of many pogroms and deportations for God's chosen). Death. Deportation. Defeat. Serbia. Bosnia. Assyria.

But God came back.

A sharp-tongued prophet, Jeremiah, promises return to the beleaguered Assyrian exiles (Jer. 31:1-6). In a speech of consolation (today's first lesson), the prophet points the way toward a great homecoming party, a great "dance of the merrymakers" (v. 4) to rival anything you've ever seen on West Campus.

Tyrants — Assyrian or any other — get edgy, nervous, call out the National Guard, whenever people on the bottom, down in the ghetto, get uppity, begin to make music, pull out tambourines, dance. And would they have ever had the guts to dance had not —

God come back?

A little backwater town in Judea, first century, Roman troops on every corner, registering these Jews, enrolling them in order better to oppress, suppress them. The greatest, most powerful army in service to the most ruthless dictator, what can anybody do? Assyrians, Romans, it's all the same. Adjust. Keep your head down. Say your prayers. But —

Down in the ghetto, in a stable out back, a young woman begins to sing. "My soul magnifies the Lord, and my spirit rejoices in God my Savior . . . he has scattered the proud. . . . He has brought down the powerful from their thrones" (Luke 1:46-47, 51-52).

Mary, why do you clinch your fist and sing? Mary replies, "Well, I'm going to have a baby."

God came back.

Friday took no one by surprise. No, if you know anything about the facts of death, the way the religio-politico-economic establishment works, then you know that he was doomed from the start. The way he disregarded social convention, eating with tax collectors, whores. The way he reached out to the wretched. The names he called the clergy! Friday's bloody business at "The Place of the Skull" comes as no surprise. You can't fight City Hall. Caesar had the troops. The crowd turned against us. The one who came inviting us all to life, now nailed to the cross, death's latest spoils of battle.

"It was a good campaign while it lasted, but we didn't get him elected Messiah," we said. We told the women, "You go on out to the cemetery and take these flowers, show our last respects to Jesus. We'll come later, when it's day." And the women went out to the city of death, peered into the tomb (Matt. 28:1-10). Surprise —

God came back.

On the way back from the cemetery (I love this) Jesus meets them and says, "Greetings!" (v. 9). And the graveyard flowers they're holding look silly, and they fall down and worship because —

God came back.

The shout of the women, you've heard it before. That day, as Pharaoh's chariots foundered and the sea surged back, in the great homecoming for exiles promised by Jeremiah, in Mary's war-chant lullaby — you've heard it before.

Greetings. God came back.

When will we become accustomed to death's defeat and the incursions of God? That the whole history of God's intrusions among us is the tale of the defeat of death's dominion? Easter is ubiquitous. When will we get it in our brains?

God came back.

That's Easter, a story begun long before Easter, a narrative not yet done with us.

God came back.

I was in East Germany when friends there — knowledge-able, university professor–type friends — declared to me: "The wall will never come down, not in our lifetime." Period. Fact. But *two weeks later* (help me, choir),

God came back.

The wall was history.

They told him, "Once a drunk, always a drunk. It's like a disease, something genetic, in your family, something in the blood, fixed." This woman whom he knew at work slipped him a note one morning. "I know what you're going through," the note said. "Been there myself. I can show you

31

a way out if you're ready to be free." I called it his AA group. He attributed it to the fact that —

God came back.

Cancer? Terminal. Untreatable. Nothing to be done, they said. Curtains. She said, "I'll *live* with it, but I'll be damned if I'm going to die of it." I called it grit. She said it was because, even in her illness,

God came back.

Her grit was more than the fruit of her emotional resilience, more than just psychological chutzpa. It arose from her Christian conviction that God is in the death dominion business, that some mighty defeat of death has been worked in the world through the resurrection of Jesus that had relevance for her struggle with death.

Who you gonna believe? The world says adjust, adapt, stuff happens. A Duke student is crushed by a bus. Pin the blame on somebody, grow up, adjust to reality, this is the way the world is.

Then the choir sings the "Hallelujah Chorus." Because — God came back!

2

Preaching as
Baptismal Encounter

The pastor baptized a baby, pouring water over the baby in the name of the Father, the Son, and the Holy Spirit, naming the baby as a Christian. Then the pastor walked down the aisle in the midst of the congregation and threw drops of water toward us, aspurging us, saying, "Remember your baptism and be thankful."

"That was strange," a fellow visitor said to me as we were walking out at the end of the service.

"Well, she does baptismal renewal that way during every baptism," I said.

"It still felt strange," said the visitor.

The more I thought about it, the more I realized how right the visitor was. Throwing water on someone in a church is strange. God forgive me for acting as if baptism were something normal. Throwing water on us and having us remember our baptism is also strange, reminding us, in word and water, of the odd way we get saved by this peculiar faith. We follow Jesus, not because it was our idea, or because we were searching for something in our lives, or because we made a study of all the world's great religions and decided that Christianity is the best. We are here because we have been encountered, assaulted, intruded upon. Just like having water splashed in our face when we are all dressed up and dignified on Sunday morning and trying desperately to look good and respectable, Jesus has intruded upon us, encountered us, made us his own. For many, that is the hoped-for message of this book: *Remember your baptism and be thankful.*

Evangelism begins in the odd, disruptive experience of being encountered by the gospel. Because the gospel is a way of thinking and being in the world that does not come naturally, we must be born again, and again. Despite the claims of those who advocate the Lamaze method of "painless birth," birth is almost never painless.

I begin with a confession. Unfortunately, one of the most dangerous moments in my preaching is when I try to appeal to the "thinking person." After all, I preach in a university chapel. A university is where people enjoy thinking of themselves as thinking people.[1]

To some of my best sermons, this is the predominant congregational response: "Well, that's *so* interesting. We'll just have to think about that. Yes we will. Fascinating way of characterizing the situation. We'll just have to think about that."

We aren't going to do a damn thing about it, but we'll just have to think about it.

My colleague Stanley Hauerwas has convinced me that, in our North American context, thinking has become a deeply problematic activity. By uncritically accommodating my preaching to "thinking," as it is presently constituted in that segment of our culture which is high-bourgeois, my preaching

1. Portions of this chapter appeared in my "Preaching to the Thinking Person's Church," in *More Sermons That Work* (Cincinnati: Forward Movement Publications, 1992).

has not only failed intellectually but also failed to do justice to the peculiar quality of thinking engendered by the gospel.

Hauerwas demonstrates that "thinking" today has become an exclusively subjective and uninformed activity — what seems right to me personally. Lacking any skills for discernment other than their own limited experience, their unformed and uninformed subjectivity, our listeners

> come to church to have confirmed what they think they already know. It is almost impossible, therefore, to resist making the sermon serve to confirm our experience rather than to challenge the presumption that we even understand what it is we assume we have experienced. Ironically, this is as true of so-called conservatives as it is of so-called liberals within the contemporary theological alternatives. Both liberals' and conservatives' strategies work to confirm different social classes' accounts of their experience. As a result, it is almost impossible for the preacher to challenge the subtle accommodationist mode of most Christian preaching. We accommodate the hearers by trying to make the sermon fit their established habits of understanding, which only underwrites the further political accommodation of the church to the status quo. Any suggestion that in order to even begin understanding the sermon would require a transformation of our lives, particularly our economic and political habits, is simply considered unthinkable.[2]

Modernity is the name for that project, begun in the European Enlightenment, which has as one of its goals to turn everyone into an individual.[3] An individual, according to the

2. Stanley Hauerwas in *Preaching to Strangers: Evangelism in Today's World* (Louisville: Westminster/John Knox Press, 1992), p. 9.
3. See my "Preaching to the Thinking Person's Church."

definitions of modernity, is someone who thinks that he or she is answerable to no story other than the one he or she has personally chosen. Determined not to be determined by tradition, family, tribe, or community, the modern person sees thinking as a matter of severing ties with the prior claims of tradition, family, and community in order to "think for myself." Earlier, people got stories from their parents, or from their church or their town, and then lived them as best they could. Adam Smith perceptively noticed that the modern world detached people from such parental determinism and enabled them to choose their own jobs, to become creators of their own lives. No longer was someone a blacksmith simply because his father was one and his name was Smith. Now we were free, free to choose; in fact, for the first time in history, writers like Adam Smith began defining freedom *as* choice.

We want to be people who have no story for our lives other than the story we have chosen. *Yet this is also a story,* and a corrupt one at that. Thanks to misleading characterizations of the views of thinkers like Immanuel Kant and Adam Smith, we are told a story that tells us that it is possible to choose our stories, to live whatever story we want. In fact, our humanity is now viewed as dependent upon our ability to choose our story. This is the "heretical imperative" that Peter Berger noted in modernity. We are all now fated to choose, to make up our own lives as we go. A life without choice is considered to be no life at all. An opinion that we have not personally thought through and chosen is considered to be unworthy of free, unconditioned human beings.

Ironically, this is also a story. We have freed ourselves from one account of wisdom only to become enslaved to another. And one of the conceits of modernity is to convince us that we are now free of stories, tradition, communities, and attachments, all the while never admitting that modernity itself is a story, a tradition (at least as old as Kant and Smith), and a very demanding, narrow story at that.

One reason why loneliness, alienation, and fragmentation appear to plague modern life is that modernity has a way of making us all strangers. When my master story is that I have no story other than the one I have personally chosen, there is little to relate me to you other than that we are both living out the story that neither of us has a common story other than the story that we ought not to harm one another's "freedom." Of course, I am not free, not half as free as I claim, for I have merely exchanged one master (the family, my hometown, my church) for another, namely, my own subjectivity. As Richard Hayes has pointed out to me, our master is even more deadly than our subjectivity. Our master is Madison Avenue. What we call our "subjectivity" is our urges and desires as manipulated by unacknowledged masters in the media and advertising. I must choose, I must serve the self, I must look out for and carefully nurture me. So all the while, thinking of ourselves as so free, we are really enslaved to ourselves and are the victims of management by strangers. We complain about the bureaucratizing of the modern nation, but as strangers who have nothing in common we need bureaucratic rules. We have given over our freedom to faceless, nameless people who write and administer rules and write TV situation comedies. As Janice Joplin sings, "Freedom's just another word for nothing left to lose."

The notion that Christian preaching must translate itself into the categories of the "thinking person" plays into the hands of this tyranny of detached subjectivity. As Hauerwas says, people come to church as individuals, thinking that their unformed subjectivity, in and of itself, qualifies them to think clearly about matters like God, Jesus, and discipleship. We come to church expecting to be confirmed in what we already know, since what we already know is, according to the canons of modernity, about all we can know. This is a peculiarly superficial way of thinking, utterly unsuited to the weirdness of the gospel.

Hauerwas often begins his classes at Duke by telling his students, "I don't want you to make up your minds about the subject matter of this course. I don't consider that you yet have minds worth making up."

By this Hauerwas means that "minds worth making up" are minds that have been formed in the skills, the habits, and the practices of knowing which enable us to think truthfully. Because "what I think" may only be a matter of my limited experience, my meager insights, my ability to delude myself, my vested economic or social interest, "what I think" may not be very interesting.

Evangelistic preaching seeks to rescue people from their unformed and uninformed subjectivity, from taking themselves too seriously in the wrong sort of way. Alas, most allegedly "evangelistic" preaching I know about is an effort to drag people even deeper into their subjectivity rather than an attempt to rescue them from it.

This spells big trouble for most of my preaching. Too much of my preaching begins at what I judge to be "where people are." I begin with their experience, their "felt need." Then, in twenty minutes, I attempt to move them to the gospel. This renders the gospel into nothing more than a helpful resource to get us what we wanted before we met the gospel. See? I have already accommodated the gospel to the assumptions of the reigning culture rather than allowed the gospel to challenge those assumptions. Evangelism is superior to apologetics because apologetics invariably concedes too much intellectual territory before the discussion begins, conceding that I know what my experiences are, what my real needs are, before I meet the gospel.

The preacher who tries to sell a congregation on the miracles of Jesus, arguing that they are "scientifically true," has lost the war before the battle begins. Point of the sermon: science is God, and everything must bow to it. The evangelist who begins a sermon with people's "felt needs" in an attempt eventually to move them toward Jesus has capitulated to the enemy without a fight. Point of the sermon: your needs, as given you by bourgeois culture, are the only thing worth having in life, and the gospel will be voted up or down on the basis of how well it relates to those needs.

The gospel is not a set of interesting ideas about which we are supposed to make up our minds. The gospel is intrusive news that evokes a new set of practices, a complex of habits, a way of living in the world, discipleship. Because of its epistemological uniqueness, we cannot merely map the gospel onto our present experiences. The gospel is not an archaic, peculiar way of naming our typical human experiences through certain religious expressions. The gospel means to engender, to evoke, a peculiar experience that we would not have had before we met the gospel.[4]

Some time ago we had a discussion at Duke University Chapel on "The Church and Homosexuality." At the end of a two-hour discussion with a panel of Christian theologians and ethicists, a young man came up to me and introduced himself as a "baptized Episcopalian" who was offended that there were no gay people on the panel. I asked him why having a gay person on the panel would make any difference, and he said it was because "I have a right to define myself, to name the significance of my own experience as a gay person."

It seemed to me that, if his first designation of himself ("I am a baptized Episcopalian") meant anything, it meant that he definitely was not to "define" himself. I knew that his church was quite explicit in its service of baptism that the church was telling him who he was, not using the conventional labels of the wider culture, labels based upon gender,

4. I have tried to base my argument here on the categories supplied by George Lindbeck in *The Nature of Doctrine: Religion and Theology in a Postliberal Age* (Philadelphia: Westminster Press, 1984).

class, race, or sexual orientation, but rather on the basis of the gospel. He was someone, in baptism, named, claimed, chosen, called. His name was "Christian."

Here is a very different way of knowing that is communal, traditional, sacramental, biblical. In our preaching, we need to help "thinking people" discover how unable they are to think, how unintelligible their lives are, when left to think for themselves. We really have no idea what is happening to us until we meet the gospel, until the gospel helps us to name our pathologies — pathologies that are so widespread in this culture as to make them appear normal — as bondage to be overcome rather than as fixed, closed reality simply to be accepted.

That's why the gospel never asks for mere intellectual agreement. The gospel call is for conversion, detoxification, rebirth. The gospel cannot be mapped onto experiences that are already there, as if the gospel can be easily transposed onto the culture of high-bourgeois narcissism. Apologetics is never as radical as evangelism because apologetics concedes too much intellectual territory to the enemy before the battle begins, adopting the culture's self-definition as the appropriate means of describing our condition. So we begin with existentialism, or self-esteem, or Marxism, or some other culturally approved category of thought and attempt to work back toward a defense of the gospel. I agree with Karl Barth that these homiletical tactics will not work because the gospel requires a severe epistemological reorientation. Our preaching to the unbaptized must aim for conversion rather than mere agreement, evangelism rather than apologetics.

Thus we can understand the waning interest in so-called inductive preaching, which begins, not with the biblical text, but rather with the hearer's experience and seeks, through the biblical text, to evoke or tap into certain aspects of that experience. Assuming that modern listeners recognize no authority other than that of their own experience, the inductive preacher bows to that authority and forms the sermon exclusively on the basis of what the preacher thinks the hearer already thinks. The listener's experience, as defined and described by the listener, is taken as preaching's point of origin. Yet this begs such questions as, When do you know you have had an "experience"? Who defines and describes experience? We have not had an experience merely because it happened to us. Interpretation precedes experience. That is, even to believe that we have had an experience is to demonstrate that we have been taught to expect certain kinds of things to happen to us.

Although Paul claimed that he received his Christian faith directly from the Lord, Paul was a Jew, and therefore he had lived in an interpretive community that had taught him to expect to be told things by God. (What he heard God telling him in Jesus' name was the big surprise!)

You and I have been initiated into a culture and a set of narratives that have told us that there is such a thing as universal, raw, uninterpreted human experience that everyone has innately and then seeks to interpret. But this is also an interpretation before it is an experience. Experience arises out of interpretation, and the gospel is a very different way of interpreting and experiencing our ethnic, gender, and economic experiences than the means of experience and interpretation offered by the predominant culture.[5]

The epistemological convictions that lie behind inductive preaching only underwrite further the political accommodation to the status quo. Modernity told us that our problem with the gospel was that it was trapped in an ancient world of outmoded authority structures (Israel and church), unavail-

5. This is my criticism of an approach to preaching such as that offered by Thomas Troeger in *A Parable of Ten Preachers* (Nashville: Abingdon Press, 1992), where racial, gender, and economic experiences, as conventionally interpreted by the categories of the majority culture, are given normative status. This is an uninteresting starting point for Christian preaching.

able experiences, and incomprehensible concepts. Historical criticism and most of the systematic theology that we learned (with the notable exception of Barth and his heirs) assured us preachers that we had a big problem of *meaning* on our hands in attempting to communicate the gospel, and that therefore our only hope for being heard was to grope for some point of contact in the present lives and understandings of our hearers. Unfortunately for such homiletics, the gospel proved to be a good deal more intellectually imperialistic than modernity knew.

The gospel knew. Our problem in "understanding" the gospel is mainly in standing under the gospel. Our intellectual problem with the gospel is not one of *meaning* but really is about power. Not the limitedly intellectual problem of "How can I believe this?" but rather "In what power configurations am I presently enslaved?"

Feminist thinkers have done us preachers a great service in showing how every intellectual claim is also a political claim, a statement about power. The need to "make up my mind" is a political matter of where power is assigned in this society. Therefore the gospel cannot be transposed into existentialism, Marxism, or the language of self-esteem without being rendered into something less than gospel. The gospel has few epistemological allies in the world, not because it is in a language so archaic as to be incomprehensible, but because the gospel seeks to reconfigure our ways of knowing, our configurations of power.

Christianity is not a description of life that everyone can understand if they just take the trouble to think about it clearly. Paul Tillich was wrong on this. The offense of the gospel is more than in the word "God"; it is that God is the Trinity, it is that Jesus Christ is Lord. Calling God "Ultimate Reality" (Tillich) is a vain attempt to sidestep the political power claim being made in biblical speech. The doctrine of original sin is not the only empirically verifiable doctrine in Christianity, self-evident to any person who knows a little Western history (Reinhold Niebuhr after Herbert Butterfield). Sin is not a mistake we make; sin is rebellion against the Trinity.

Christianity, we believe, is not a story we have chosen, something about which we have decided. It chose us. We have been embraced by this story from outside of our limited experiences. This is an "external word" (Luther) that someone had to speak to us ("Faith comes from what is heard," said Paul in Romans 10:17) in order for us to discover it. So in a sense, we don't discover the gospel, it discovers us. "You did not choose me but I chose you" (John 15:16).

Inductive preaching, too much so-called narrative preaching in which I "share my story," a great deal of liberation preaching in which I am urged to "theologize from my experience of oppression," and much psychologized preaching in which I am told that the gospel is some sort of psychic solution to something that ailed me before I came to church — all assume that I am already equipped to hear and to receive the gospel just as I am. No. I must be trained to hear the gospel, to ask the right questions for which it is the answer. A lifetime of skills will be required, constant correction by my brothers and sisters in the church, confession, forgiveness, worship. In fact, I once defined Christian worship as "learning to pay attention." I stick by that definition. It is no easy thing to learn to pay more attention to God and less to myself. I therefore need to worship habitually, every Sunday, in morning and evening prayer, so distracting is my world.

The gospel is more odd than we liberal mainliners care to admit, certainly more odd than the conservative fundamentalists admit. Conflict is inevitable when the gospel challenges the power configurations in which we find ourselves. Sparks fly. There is struggle that is considerably more disruptive than the mere nod of intellectual assent. None of us understands this gospel until we stand under it. We were born in bloody

Exodus, after all. We became family after an unmarried woman gave birth and Herod slaughtered the boy babies.

*   *   *

> Then Jesus said to the disciples, "There was a rich man who had a manager, and charges were brought to him that this man was squandering his property. So he summoned him and said to him, 'What is this that I hear about you? Give me an accounting of your management, because you cannot be my manager any longer.' Then the manager said to himself, 'What will I do, now that my master is taking the position away from me? I am not strong enough to dig, and I am ashamed to beg. I have decided what to do so that, when I am dismissed as manager, people may welcome me into their homes.' So, summoning his master's debtors one by one, he asked the first, 'How much do you owe my master?' He answered, 'A hundred jugs of olive oil.' He said to him, 'Take your bill, sit down quickly, and make it fifty.' Then he asked another, 'And how much do you owe?' He replied, 'A hundred containers of wheat.' He said to him, 'Take your bill and make it eighty.' And his master commended the dishonest manager. . . .

Luke 16:1-8a

This is the most outrageous of Jesus' parables. Here is a rich man who calls in his manager, accuses him of bilking him out of his money, and demands that he pay up right now what he owes. The manager, thinking to himself what a lowlife he really is, how unsuited he would be for honest work, scurries about, doctors up the master's books, talks the master's debtors into conspiring with him, and then presents his master with the money that he owes, money that he has obtained through some hook and a lot of crook.

44

And the master *commended* the dishonest manager.

This story has caused problems for the church ever since it was told by Jesus. Some have tried to deny that Jesus told it. Augustine wondered aloud, Could a story as sleazy as this come from the mouth of Jesus? Perhaps it was inserted into the New Testament by somebody else. Forget it. If we were inserting stuff into the Bible, do you think we would have inserted this? No, the parable's very outrageousness is proof of its utter authenticity.

The *Living Bible* paraphrase has Jesus say something like, "Do you think the Master would commend the dishonest steward? No!"

Nice try, *Living Bible*.

No. It says what it says. The master really did praise the shenanigans of a dishonest steward.

So, whose side are you on? Who is the good guy here? This is church. We often come to church looking for examples to follow, ways to live better lives, trying to be good.

Who is the good guy here?

The rich man? No. He's *rich*. Enough said. He's the boss who lives in the big house overlooking the shanties behind his mill. While others slave over his looms, he sits beside his pool moving stocks by cellular telephone. We're never on his side. Our sympathy is always with the little guy. We loved *Ferris Buehler's Day Off*, when he put the principal in his place. And we all went to see Robin Hood fleece the rich in order to give to the poor. We love stories where the rich go down and the little guy goes up.

A couple of years ago, the worst labor disaster in North Carolina history occurred in Hamlet, North Carolina. Over a dozen poultry plant workers died in a fire, trapped behind locked doors. A member of the occupational safety commission said, "This disaster was partly the fault of the workers themselves. The exit doors had to be locked because some of the workers stole chickens." How much is a chicken worth?

Somebody's mother died because a worker on minimum wage stole a couple of Mr. Big's chickens?

If some little guy, some Robin Hood, wants to put one over on the boss, fine!

Which means that, not being on the side of the rich man, you are on the side of the manager, the *unjust* manager. He won our sympathy from the very first, when the boss called him in and said, "Give account of your stewardship or get out!" Standing there, poor little thing, trembling in his boots before the man behind the big oak desk, we're on his side.

"What am I to do?" he says to himself. And now his character begins to emerge. He is accused of "wasting" his master's money. Wasting, *diaskorpizein,* the same word used for what the Prodigal Son did with his dad's money out in the far country.[6] He blew it. Wasted it. It isn't like this guy has been using that money to feed his wife and children, to provide for the kids' education, or to support his poor, sick mother. He wasted it. Now, he'll have to pay up or get out.

"What am I to do? I'm too lazy to do honest work like digging, and I'm too proud to beg." He has been putting on airs, living high through his master's money for so long that the thought of falling backwards into poverty is more than he can bear. His master drives a Mercedes, and he drives a fully loaded Buick. His master has a place in Palm Springs, and he has a condo at Myrtle Beach. He isn't about to give that up.

So he calls in those who owe his master. The swindle begins. "Master, I'll be happy to turn in the books to you after a few . . . er, uh . . . *adjustments.*"

He calls in one debtor who owes the master twenty thousand bucks. "Change your bill," he tells him. "Make it

6. My thanks to Robert Farrar Capon for this insight and for his playful, yet penetrating analysis of this parable in *The Parables of Grace* (Grand Rapids: Eerdmans, 1988), pp. 145-51.

ten and give me five." Large amounts are being written off here.

This little Robin Hood whom you loved so much at the beginning of the story is turning out to be a Jim Bakker. He's not robbing from the rich to help the poor; he's fleecing widows in order to maintain his heated doghouse and mirror-ceilinged bedroom.

He is the Pentagon general who allows defense contractors to overcharge the government so that, when he retires from government work, he can get a plush job as a consultant with that same contractor. This is Imelda Marcos stashing her people's money away in Swiss bank accounts for a rainy day.

This is the person with whom you identified in the story? I am shocked. I thought you were all good people. A lazy, thieving, cheating, disloyal liar? You were on *his* side?

We love to see the rich get clobbered. We love getting even, yes. But lies? Cheating? Stealing? You said you liked Robin Hood. If you approve of that sort of stealing, it isn't too far to this sort of stealing. But aren't you ashamed? And in church too? In one of Jesus' own parables to boot?

"And his master commended the dishonest manager." End of story. The master has moved in this story from "You crook, you! Turn over your books or get out" to "You genius, you! A crooked genius but still a genius."

We have now flip-flopped through this parable worse than George Bush's civil-rights policy. Like a ping-pong ball, first we were on the side of the manager against the master, then, the more we got to know this sleazy manager, we were over with the master against the steward, and now, by the end of the story, after the master has praised the crookedness of the manager, we have had it with them both. Two birds of a feather.[7]

---

7. I have been helped in my interpretation by Bernard Brandon Scott, *Hear Then the Parable* (Minneapolis: Fortress Press, 1989), pp. 255-66.

That manager should have been fired or worse. Lies and deceit earn him his master's praise. You said you were on the side of the manager when we began this parable. Do you think cheating is okay? Well, no! (Well, only if it's with the IRS or in Algebra 1.) What kind of person are you? Forget the manager and the master, what kind of person are *you?*[8]

At first we believed that the rich man is bad (after all, he's rich), and the manager is good (after all, he's like us). Then the manager upsets our moral order through his laziness and conniving, and we're back on the side of the master.

"I can see what you've been putting up with all these years with this guy," we say to the boss. "You should have fired him long ago! I can see it your way now!"

Then, just when we get it all figured out, all tied down — the good separated from the bad, the wheat from the chaff, the saved from the damned, the in from the out — this master goes and *praises* this crooked manager, for heaven's sake.

We grope through this parable, looking for Mr. Goodbar, groping around to find just one good person with whom we can identify (one good person like us), only to have this parable jump us from behind and nab us. What kind of people are we to approve, condone, justify, and identify with such people? Who are we?

My colleague Dan Via has noted that a parable is like a window. We encounter a parable like this one as if looking through a window, looking out at the world. What sort of world do you see through this window? A world of cheats and scoundrels in high and low places, wheeling and dealing by the rich and the poor?

8. My colleague Richard Lischer has noted that historical criticism has taught the mainline church to deal with a biblical text by stepping back from the text. The African-American church, on the other hand, learned that the best way to understand a biblical text is to step into the text.

Yet sometimes, looking through a window, there is that moment when the window becomes a mirror and you become conscious of your own reflection in the window. You see yourself.

Too often we think of religion as a means of sticking labels on other people, labels reading "the good" and "the bad." But by the end of the story, we all get stuck. We want to use Scripture as a knife to cut cleanly between the victims and the villains, and Scripture has become a two-edged sword. We assumed that the rich man was bad, simply because he was rich and we are not. Now, we're confused. And we don't like to be confused, not in church.

The Kingdom is a time of accounting in this parable and in so many others, a time to settle accounts, to face facts, to look at the books. And when we do, in the searching light of Bible honesty, we find that *we may be no worse, but we are certainly no better, than they.* We condoned injustice. Doesn't the master clearly say that the manager is "dishonest"? Alas, we are the master of lies and the manager of deceit.

A recent study by the Lilly Foundation, after questioning hundreds of young adults, says that contemporary young adults are looking for a church with "clear moral norms." Yet this parable has cut us loose from our moral moorings, set us adrift in a sea of relativity where people don't act as we expect. The story dislocates us; it provides no answers, only accusing questions.

The parable has made us think (something we don't like to do in church!), think of other stories that are equally disruptive, like the story about the wasteful son who, after squandering his father's inheritance, drags himself home in rags, smelling of booze and the cheap perfume of harlots, and the father . . . *throws a party.* Like the story about a man bleeding in a ditch, passed by the good people, helped only by this morally suspect Samaritan.

Such thinking provokes a crisis, and this crisis is one of the first moves to be made in evangelical preaching. Years ago Reuel Howe chided preachers for sermons that are long on analysis and short on solution, big on crisis and short on resolution, leaving frustrated listeners.[9] I ask, What's wrong with crisis? Is the good news of the gospel a resolution to our problems, or is it the beginning of problems we would gladly have avoided if left to our own devices? Too much that passes for evangelistic preaching is the preaching of resolutions and solutions — "Come to Jesus and get fixed." Yet this parable, with its utterly unsatisfying conclusion, its provocation of troubling questions, suggests that evangelistic preaching is a monkey wrench thrown into the clanking machinery of our solutions and our management of ourselves before God.

Where are you in this story? I am the manager, managing my morals, wheeling and dealing, looking out for Number One, willing to cheat if it will help. I am the master, condoning immoral behavior, secretly admiring the shrewd scoundrels of this world. As a preacher, I can't afford to be too tough on *your* behavior because mine is nothing to write home about.

Even my liberal, open-minded self-satisfaction that at least *I* am not guilty of using the gospel as a means of stabilization and smug self-righteousness (unlike all those simple-minded fundamentalists!) is evidence of my smug self-righteousness. Few in my university congregation come to church to be assured that Jesus has fixed them. Rather, they come to be assured that the way they are fixed — in their presumed liberal open-mindedness — is the way Jesus intends them to be fixed. Self-salvation is the goal of much of our preaching.

Luther said that a sermon is best as "the thunderbolt by means of which God with one blow destroys both open sinners and false saints."

9. Reuel Howe, *Partners in Preaching* (New York: Seabury Press, 1967), pp. 27-28.

Last year, watching a television special on the outbreak of bank robberies in Los Angeles, my righteous indignation burned hot within me as I watched the films of banks being robbed by masked gunmen. Something like a dozen banks are robbed every day in Los Angeles. "They ought to do something about it," I thought to myself. Those bank robbers.

An FBI agent discussing the robberies said, "We are deeply concerned about this epidemic of bank robbery. It's a wonder that so few people have gotten killed. Of course, bank robbery is a particularly stupid crime since about eighty percent of all bank robbers are eventually caught, a much higher percentage of conviction than with most other crimes. We get the whole thing on tape. A high percentage of them are mothers on heroin."

Then he said something that gave me pause. "Comparatively little money is lost in bank robberies, no more than a couple hundred thousand dollars last year in California. That's not much money lost compared with the money lost in the Savings and Loan swindles. The taxpayers have had to come up with billions to pay for that one. Of course, unlike our bank robbers, those guys all wear expensive three-piece suits and work in the office upstairs, and unlike our bank robbers, few of those guys will ever go to jail."

I had met the criminal, and to my surprise, he looked like me. Luther said, "The glory of the grace of God is to make us enemies of ourselves."

We have met the scoundrel, and he is us. Our face is all over this story. We really are a moral mess. We really do need someone to save us, someone who is not too respectable, for we certainly are not. We could use a crook like us. And he was. He broke the Sabbath. He consorted and partied with crooks and harlots. He outraged the scholars in the department of religion. He died, a criminal on either side, as a crook himself.

A respectable savior could never have loved and saved a

crowd of rogues like us. He became one of us in order to save us. He lowered moral standards and disrupted respectable ethical order. He said he came to settle up accounts between us and God. So we got all cleaned up, put on a coat and tie, and scrambled to the front pew at church in hopes of doctoring up our books. He looked, in the end, upon all our wheeling and dealing that so neatly nailed him to the cross, he looked upon us who deserved to be clobbered for our crookedness, high and low, and clobbered us with his grace, high and low, saying, "Father, forgive."

Salvation is not just a state of existence made possible by the work of Jesus. Salvation *is* Jesus. It is the willingness to listen to and follow along behind Jesus, the intention to be part of the people whom he invites to his table.

To be a Christian is to be part of the community, the countercultural community, formed by thinking with a peculiar story. The story is *euangelion, good* news, because it is about grace. Yet it is also *news* because it is not common knowledge, not what nine out of ten average Americans already know. Gospel doesn't come naturally. It comes as Jesus.

> That I may rise and stand, o'erthrow me, and bend
> Your force to break, blow, burn, and make me new.

(John Donne, *Holy Sonnet 14*)

Which reminds us of a story from the Damascus road.

"The God of the Second Chance"

Third Sunday of Easter
Acts 9:1-20

"Saul got up from the ground, and though his eyes were open, he could see nothing; so they led him by the hand. . . ."

Acts 9:8

I know a student, a senior, who ran afoul of the rules, did wrong, and was called before the dean to answer for his misbehavior. He thought he was going to be kicked out of school. The dean acted in mercy. After some penance, the student was allowed to resume his studies. I saw him the next day.

"I feel like a freshman," he confided.

"Why's that?" I asked. "Because what you did was so stupid?"

"No," he said, "because I'm starting all over again. I've been given a second chance."

A second chance is no small thing. In a recent book on the life of Dr. Billy Graham,* William Martin says that the

---

*A Prophet with Honor: The Billy Graham Story (New York: William Morrow, 1991).

primary reason for Dr. Graham's lifelong, phenomenal success is that Graham has consistently preached "the transforming power of a second chance." Dr. Graham's own life demonstrates the change he has preached to others in his own dramatic changes of heart on nuclear disarmament, communism, racism. Billy Graham has consistently preached, as the one lasting solution to all personal and social ills, transforming commitment to Jesus Christ. Martin shows that the majority of the thousands of inquirers who have come forward at Graham's crusades are not really first-time converts but "rededicators." Yet Martin asks, "Is a rededication of one's life to Christ any less momentous than a first-time conversion?" A second chance, early or late, is no small thing.

And surely the paradigmatic, Billy Graham, evangelical, Christian story of the second chance is today's Scripture: the conversion of Saul. Most of us know the story of Saul's conversion on the Damascus road so well that we hardly need to retell it. Or do we?

We first met Saul back in the seventh chapter of Acts where Luke calls him "a young man" who watched over the garments of those who were stoning Stephen to death. Very quickly this Saul moves from being a willing bystander to an active persecutor of Christians. "Saul was ravaging the church by entering house after house; dragging off both men and women, he committed them to prison" (8:3). Saul is a busy, resourceful, dangerous Enemy Number One of the church. By the time we meet him again here in chapter 9, Saul has gotten himself appointed head of the Stop-the-Church Movement. He has official letters granting him power from the authorities in his program of persecution. He's on his way to Damascus to stamp out this Christian thing once and for all.

Later Christian preachers have imagined Saul's possible inner turmoil, his possible doubts about his mission, which may have led to his conversion. They have had him searching for something more fulfilling in his life, something that might better explain how this story ends in conversion. Forget it. There's none of that in the story. Saul isn't searching for anything except Christians. He isn't filled with inner doubts or uncertainty. He has no doubts at all about the will of God and what he ought to be doing with his life. He is a full-time theological authority, *a big man,* conducting investigations, holding court, helping to make Israel safe again for God.

On the road to Damascus, he hears his name called: "Saul, Saul." He doesn't know the one who calls him. But the voice intrudes, devastates his self-confident journey. In an instant, the once vibrant, intelligent, believing, sure, resourceful man is rendered helpless. He opens his eyes, but he can't see. He has to be led around by the hand by strangers like Ananias, and he can't eat or drink for three days.

It's quite a contrast to the Saul we first met, Mr. Big Believer, the one who was so active, going to and fro with letters of introduction from the bigwigs up at the temple, pursuing believers all the way to Damascus. Now, he is helpless, frail, needy, small — *like a little child.* He has reverted, fallen backwards toward . . . a second life. His turnaround was so dramatic that his old name would not do. In baptism, he got a new name for his new life — Paul.

Earlier, on another road, the one leading toward Jerusalem and a cross (Luke 18:15-17), Jesus began to teach people concerning his kingdom. Everyone was listening, everyone trying to pay attention, taking notes. And there were these children there. Someone had pulled someone else's hair. Two were rolling in the dirt. Another was marking up a hymnal with a crayon. The disciples said, "Send these children away! We can't pay attention to the serious, grown-up, religious business with these children here! Don't we have a nursery or 'Children's Church' or something for these children?"

You remember what Jesus did? He called for the children; he said, "Let the children come to me. Don't stop them. For it is to such as these that the Kingdom of God belongs. You can never enter God's kingdom unless you come as a little child."

Saul, who once knew so much about religion, about God, about big, important ideas and big, significant people, is rendered by the blinding light on the Damascus road into a little child who must be led by the hand, healed at the mercy of strangers, instructed by the very ones he once thought he was above. Here is a strange path of enlightenment in which we progress by regression and go forward by falling backward, and there is confusion, speechlessness, hunger, and childish crawling toward light.

Saul was so completely changed by the intruding voice of God that he now answered to a different name: Paul. Church Public Enemy Number One became Number One Leader of the Church. God had made a very big move with Saul.

Every big move in life has some common themes. There must be detachment from old certainties and securities, with the accompanying experience of dislocation and anomie, some rootlessness and confusion. Paul wanders about stumbling, blind. And we don't like that. We want to be big, in control, calling the shots. We want to take sure steps toward the world, the right steps on the right road, letters of introduction, a Duke diploma, all grown up. Wanting to control all of life's moves, we don't make too many big moves.

I was talking to this student. A senior here, just before graduation. I asked him, "Are you religious?"

"I used to be," he answered. "I was taken to church when I was a kid. I guess everybody is, when they are kids. But now that I've come to college, matured, I just don't feel the need of religion anymore. The way I see it, religion is like training wheels on a kid's bike. It's fine, until you get your bearings, can think for yourself, stand on your own two feet. Then, you don't need religion anymore."

Training wheels! That's all faith is for.

But life, being what it is, may take us on some circuitous

paths, some of them leading down. And we won't get into God's kingdom except as a little child. This paradigmatic story of Saul invites us to ask: Must we be blinded before we can see light? Must we experience belittlement before we can really grow up?

Is this why, every year or so, I always read a novel by Dostoyevsky? In his novels, *Crime and Punishment, The Brothers Karamazov,* Dostoyevsky loves to take a person — self-sufficient, intelligent, knowledgeable, competent — and break him down, piece by piece, bit by bit, until in the end he is nothing more than a whimpering, out of control, small child. Only then is there light, redemption.

A second chance, early or late in life, is not cheap. And we can never enter *this* kingdom, except as a little child.

*   *   *

This past summer, a lifelong friend of mine hit bottom, spun out of control, crossed the median, headed the wrong way down the interstate at 100 miles an hour. In other words, he fell from his prestigious perch as an attorney to the depths of alcoholism.

The good news is, he is on his way back, thanks to his loving wife and children and the good work of Alcoholics Anonymous. (Acts 9 shows that nobody gets born again by himself.)

Among the many things that surprised him, on his way back to life, was church. He had always gone to church, but like many smart people, he always considered himself a step or so above it all. Church was for losers, for intellectual wimps. Training wheels. Church was for folk without the intellectual equipment to think for themselves.

"You would be amazed at what I've learned about God," said my friend.

"Like what?" I asked.

"So many words I had heard all my life in church have suddenly, like a flash of blinding light, become real to me," he said. "Words, little Christian slogans, that I've heard all my life, are suddenly, amazingly real, deep, blindingly true."

"Like what?" I asked.

"Like being 'born again.' Or like 'you can only find your life by losing it.' Or, say, like 'take up your cross daily and follow me.' Through my pain, by hitting bottom, I've met God," said my friend.

"And who is the God you have met?" I asked.

"God is a tough, relentless, devastating friend," he said, "who won't have us until we are down on our knees, whimpering like a baby, so weak, stupid, and helpless, that I don't know whether I've been born or I've died."

Something like scales fell from his eyes. His sight was restored. He got up and was baptized. He took food and regained his strength.

So now you know why, when a student recently told me that since she had come to Duke — thought deeply about things, taken a religion course, majored in philosophy — she had been able to put God behind her, grow up, and live her life quite well without recourse to such infantile notions as God, I said, "Great, give it a try. Get all grown up and liberated and adult and fossilized if you wish. But as you journey, you better keep looking back over your shoulder."

*　　　*　　　*

It is no small thing to have been loved by the God of the second chance.*

---

*For exegetical insights, see my *Acts: A Commentary for Teaching and Preaching* (Atlanta: John Knox Press, 1983), pp. 71-79, 100-104; and Beverly R. Gaventa, *From Darkness to Light: Aspects of Conversion in the New Testament* (Philadelphia: Fortress Press, 1986). Marvelous anthropological insights into the nature of conversion as a widespread human experience can be found in Hans J. Mol, *Identity and the Sacred* (New York: Macmillan, 1977).

3

Making Room for God

Christian evangelism arises within the gaps between God and ourselves, not with our conventional ways of bridging the gap, but with God's ways.

I'll admit that such thinking about evangelical preaching is new for me. When I was in seminary, someone told us that the preacher stands in the pulpit with the Bible in one hand and today's newspaper in the other. In twenty minutes, the preacher seeks to bring these two disparate worlds together. Someone said that Barth said it, though it doesn't sound like Barth and I have never found it in his writings. Even if the sainted Barth said it, the metaphor is wrong. The preacher laboring to bring together the archaic, irrelevant world of the Bible with the relevant, new world of today is a problematic image considering our ways of bridging the gap, our ways of construing the gap. If we think of the gap between us and God, we characterize it as a problem of time, a problem of history, when more likely our greatest communicative problem with the gospel is a problem of our idolatry. To be brought, through a sermon, into the presence of the living God is to be made aware of a gap, a gap between us and God that has little to do with the two-thousand-year interval between us and the Bible.

The gap is there because we are unaccustomed to looking at the living God.

We preachers, often in the interest of a misguided evangelism, are forever guilty of attempting inappropriately to bridge that gap, to domesticate the gospel, to housebreak God, producing a gospel that is honey to make the world's solutions go down easier, rather than salt or light. In fact, evangelistic preaching is deemed to be that preaching which renders the gospel "user friendly," the reduction of the gospel to a slogan for a bumper sticker, a church billboard.

Earlier I recalled how, years ago, Reuel Howe interviewed laypeople and asked them what they thought about preaching. Howe's most frequently heard lay complaint was that sermons were too long on analysis of problems and too short on solutions. People want sermons that, in twenty minutes or less, somehow provide resolution to life's conflicts, answers to our questions, solutions.[1]

The gospel is answer to our deepest questions, solution to our most pressing problems. Yet before it is answer, it is question. Or should we say that within the gospel's answer is the provocation of our most perplexing questions?[2] If this be God, in the presence of this Jew from Nazareth, then who are we? How then should we live? What is going on in the world?

Too often popular American evangelism presents the gospel as the solution to all our problems, the resolution of all conflict, another technique for making nice people even nicer, successful people even more successful.

"My life was a mess. I was on drugs. I was addicted to

---

1. Reuel Howe, *Partners in Preaching* (New York: Seabury Press, 1967), pp. 25-30.
2. Earlier, in my book *The Gospel for the Person Who Has Everything* (Valley Forge, PA: Judson Press, 1977), I knew that something was wrong with our evangelistic preaching, but I did not know as much about what was biblically wrong with it as I know now.

sex. I ate high cholesterol snacks. Then I found Jesus . . . and everything got fixed."

Against the notion of evangelism as simplification of the gospel to the point where no one could raise objections, accommodation of the gospel to the unformed and uninformed limits of our listeners, I would like to plead for another way, a way that sees the prime evangelistic moment, not in resolution and solution, but in the gap, the gap between us and God, as well as the peculiar way in which God deals with that gap in Jesus Christ.

Gerhard Ebeling once said that "Theology is necessary in order to make preaching as hard for the preacher as it has to be."[3] Whenever preaching gets easy — an oversimplification of the gospel into rules for better living, proverbial wisdom with a dash of pop psychology, Leo Buscaglia dressed up like Jesus — theology comes along and pushes preaching to be more faithful. What Ebeling claims for theology ought also to be true for the relationship of biblical interpretation to preaching. Encounter with Scripture keeps reminding preaching that it does not own God, that it has not fully described the God of Abraham, Isaac, Jacob, Mary, and Jesus in its span of twenty minutes. Theology helps preaching to keep the gaps open, to keep the space between the pulpit and the throne of God free, untamed, threatening, and interesting.

We had this recruiter for the "Teach America" program, the program that attempts to recruit bright young prospective teachers from college and university campuses to teach in America's most difficult and deprived school systems. To an auditorium full of Duke students, she said, "Looking at you tonight, I don't know why I'm here. You are privileged, the beneficiaries of the best of this nation's educational resources. I can tell, just by looking at you, that you are all bound for Wall Street, law

3. Gerhard Ebeling, *Word and Faith* (Philadelphia: Fortress Press, 1963), p. 424.

school, med. school. And here I stand, trying to recruit you for a salary of $15,000 a year in some of the worst school situations in America, begging you to waste your life for a bunch of ungrateful kids in the backwoods of Appalachia or the inner city of Philadelphia. I must have been crazy to come here.

"But I do have some literature up here, and I would be willing to talk to anybody who happens to be interested. But I know, just by looking at you, that all of you want to be a success, and here I am inviting you to be failures. So you can all leave now. But if by chance somebody here feels called to do the worst job any of you can imagine, then I'm here to talk to you. The meeting's over."

With that, everyone stood up and stampeded to the front, fighting over a chance to talk to this recruiter, just dying to give their lives to something more interesting than conventional American success, dying to give themselves to something bigger and more important than themselves.

Her tough challenge to prospective teachers reminded me of Richard Lovelace's peculiar call to evangelism:

> We may need to challenge more, and comfort less, in our evangelism and discipleship. We need to make it harder for people to retain assurance of salvation when they move into serious sin. . . . [W]e need to tell some persons who think they have gotten saved to get lost. The Puritans were biblically realistic about this; we have become sloppy and sentimental in promoting assurance under any circumstances.[4]

We preachers often try to get too close to our listeners, to bridge the gap, to make it all sound easy. There is something to be said for making it sound too difficult.

4. Richard Lovelace, "Evangelicalism: Recovering a Tradition of Spiritual Depth," *The Reformed Journal,* September 1990, p. 25.

One reason why we preachers talk so much, why we can be justly accused on Sunday morning of "diarrhea of the mouth," is that we appear to be terrified by empty spaces in Sunday worship. We fill all the gaps with words, mindless chatter, running commentary for the congregation. "Let's now stand and sing that great hymn by Charles Wesley 'O for a Thousand Tongues to Sing,' let us stand as we sing. . . ."

Why are we so afraid of the gaps? Is it because, in our pastoral heart of hearts, we know that it is in the silence, in the gaps, that God might come, might shatter our polite bourgeois arrangements and blow us to bits? Thus C. S. Lewis advises that, to avoid God successfully, one must keep every moment filled and avoid any space, any gaps, at all cost:

> Avoid silence, avoid solitude, avoid any train of thought that leads off the beaten track. Concentrate on money, sex, status, health and (above all) on your own grievances. Keep the radio on. Live in a crowd. Use plenty of sedation. If you must read books, select them very carefully. But you'd be safer to stick to the papers. You'll find the advertisements helpful; especially those with a sexy or a snobbish appeal.[5]

Or, as Lewis's devil Screwtape puts it, all of space and time in hell is occupied by noise: "Noise, the grand dynamism, the audible expression of all that is exultant, ruthless, and virile — Noise which alone defends us from silly qualms, despairing scruples, and impossible desires. We will make the whole universe a noise in the end."[6] Hell is that place

5. C. S. Lewis, "The Seeing Eye," in *Christian Reflections,* ed. Walter Hooper (Grand Rapids: Eerdmans, 1967), pp. 168-69.

6. C. S. Lewis, *The Screwtape Letters* (New York: Macmillan, 1982), pp. 102-3.

where Muzak is always playing full blast so that there is never room left for the words of God.

> Where shall the word be found, where will the word
>   resound?
> Not here, there is not enough silence.

> T. S. Eliot, "Ash Wednesday"

After twenty years of thinking of preaching as my attempt to close the gap, I now conceive of preaching, faithful evangelical preaching, as opening up the gap. For it is in the gaps, the great big frightening, invigorating gaps, that we can wander, reenvision, reform, be reborn. When preachers try to fill all the gaps with our suggestions for better living, our solutions to the world's problems, there is no space left for God to come and save us. God must have room.

Myth and Parable

How to construe the gap that is the by-product of faithful preaching? Biblical scholar John Dominic Crossan, in his book *The Dark Interval,* makes a distinction between *myth* and *parable.* Myth, says Crossan, attempts to mediate opposites, explain mystery, reconcile polarities, to take the randomness of life and weave it into a believable pattern. In myth, bad guys get what they deserve, and the good are rewarded. Through myth, there are explanations for the apparent incongruities of life, reasons given by the gods.

Why is there evil in the world? Well, this *woman,* Pandora, you know how nosey women are, wouldn't stay in her place, opened the mysterious box, and evil and heartache were unleashed on the world. That's why there's evil in the world. Any more questions?

64

Myth explains, settles, closes the gaps in our consciousness.

Crossan says myth's polar opposite is *parable*. "Parable brings not peace but the sword, . . . parable casts fire upon the earth."[7] Literary critic Frank Kermode says, "Myths are the agents of stability, fictions the agents of change."[8] Parable is meant to change us, not reassure us. Parable is always a somewhat unnerving experience. The standard reaction to parable is "I don't know what you mean by that story, but I'm certain I don't like it."

Crossan argues that myth has as its function the creation of a belief in the possibility of permanent reconciliation between the polarities and contradictions that bedevil us. Parable hopes to create contradiction within our complacent securities. "You have built a lovely home, myth assures us; but, whispers parable, you are right above an earthquake fault."[9] Myth establishes world. Parable subverts world. Parable creates humility by reminding us of limits, by enticing us right up to the very edge of certitude, forcing us to peer over into the terrifying abyss of a world we do not know.

Now Jesus' primary, and certainly most distinctive, mode of communication was parable. What do we evangelists make of that? Jesus did not talk primarily in allegory, did not preach three-point sermons, did not offer little moralistic messages. He told parables.

In most any parable, there is a reversal of expectation, a dislocation of the hearer. Right there, at the point where conventional expectations are reversed, where the listener is dislodged, dislocated, right there is the evangelical moment, there where God has room to move upon us and upon our

7. John Dominic Crossan, *The Dark Interval* (Sonoma, CA: Polebridge Press, 1988), p. 38.
8. Crossan, p. 39.
9. Crossan, p. 40.

present constructions of reality. Preachers who would be evangelical ought to delight in such moments, moments when parable has its way with us and we are cut loose.

For instance, one of the most dearly beloved of Jesus' parables (beloved by preachers, that is) is the apocalypse in Matthew 25:31-46. I loved it because it appeared in the former Methodist lectionary, a one-year lectionary that always offered this parable at just the right time of the year — the fall stewardship campaign. "Lord, when did we see you?" was my rhetorical question in the sermon. "I'll tell you when we saw him. When we looked at this year's church budget and saw that it was ten percent over last year's. Inasmuch as you have raised your pledge ten percent, you have done it unto the 'least of these.'"

It was a good sermon. Adaptable too. All the preacher had to do was to fill in whatever cause appealed most to the preacher — prison reform in North Carolina, voting a straight Democratic ticket in the upcoming election, increased giving to the church — and say that was the way in which we helped the "least of these," the means whereby we helped Jesus, the means by which we shall be judged.

Although this interpretation led to some wonderful sermons, they were mostly sermons based upon myth rather than parable, the solution of tensions through myth rather than the enjoyment of them in parable. Is this a moralistic story in which Jesus warns us to get ourselves right with God by visiting the prisoner, giving a cup of cold water, or voting right in the next election? I once thought that to be the correct interpretive approach. Now, I see otherwise.

> "When the Son of Man comes in his glory, and all the angels with him, then he will sit on the throne of his glory. All the nations will be gathered before him, and he will separate people one from another as a shepherd separates

the sheep from the goats, and he will put the sheep at his right hand and the goats at the left. Then the king will say to those at his right hand, 'Come, you that are blessed by my Father, inherit the kingdom prepared for you from the foundation of the world; for I was hungry and you gave me food, I was thirsty and you gave me something to drink, I was a stranger and you welcomed me, I was naked and you gave me clothing, I was sick and you took care of me, I was in prison and you visited me.' Then the righteous will answer him, 'Lord, when was it that we saw you hungry and gave you food, or thirsty and gave you something to drink? And when was it that we saw you a stranger and welcomed you, or naked and gave you clothing? And when was it that we saw you sick or in prison and visited you?' And the king will answer them, 'Truly I tell you, just as you did it to one of the least of these who are members of my family, you did it to me.' Then he will say to those at his left hand, 'You that are accursed, depart from me into the eternal fire prepared for the devil and his angels; for I was hungry and you gave me no food, I was thirsty and you gave me nothing to drink, I was a stranger and you did not welcome me, naked and you did not give me clothing, sick and in prison and you did not visit me.' Then they also will answer, 'Lord, when was it that we saw you hungry or thirsty or a stranger or naked or sick or in prison, and did not take care of you?' Then he will answer them, 'Truly I tell you, just as you did not do it to one of the least of these, you did not do it to me.' And these will go away into eternal punishment, but the righteous into eternal life.'"

Matthew 25:31-46

Some time ago, Leander Keck of Yale Divinity School, in a Bible study on this passage, after hearing our interpretation of the passage, asked us preachers, "What is the emotional tone of this parable? Don't ask yourself, 'What does this say?' Ask yourself, 'What does this parable do?'"

Then I remembered hearing this parable as a child. Back then, before my parabolic interpretation had become corrupted by courses at Yale Divinity School, the thing that impressed me was how stupid everyone was in this parable. Yes, how dumb. One expected the goats to be dumb. After all, not having been to church and Sunday school, the goats were outsiders. They weren't supposed to know Jesus when they saw him.

Yet the surprising thing about the parable, at least to me at ten years old, was how dumb the sheep were. They didn't know any more than the goats, couldn't see Jesus when he stood before them as "the least of these."

Then I realized how my preaching had perverted the parable. I had preached this perfectly outrageous parable in such a way as to enfeeble it. Unintentionally, I had blasphemously preached, "Don't let the Judge put one over on you at the Great Judgment. Do what I tell you in this sermon and you can escape judgment — vote right, give right, do right."

No, the parable says clearly, We shall be judged. And the shock is that we shall be judged by criteria other than those of our own devising. We shall be judged by the one whose "ways are higher than our ways, whose thoughts are deeper than our thoughts" (Isa. 55:9). We shall be shocked, in the end, by how differently God judges things from the way we judge things. And nothing I do as a preacher ought to soften the shock of the story.

As an evangelical preacher, I am to bring people before the living God, not to protect people from God. I am to leave them free to wander, to explore the space between us and the throne. I am to frustrate their desires to relax the tension between our ways and God's ways.

Surprise. We come to church expecting to get put right,

located in a secure world of righteousness, only to be dislodged by the parable. What is the function of religion if not to "get us right with God"? Maybe its true function is to leave us alone with God. Luther advised us preachers to interpret the Scripture in such a way that people are stripped naked, driven into the arms of a gracious God, bereft of our allegedly righteous props and posturing.

As Crossan says, parables enhance our consciousness of ignorance, which may be the beginning of true wisdom. The beginning of salvation is the subversion of all salvation. The beginning of being found is to be lost. The beginning of finding is losing, dislocation. Parables are a first step toward evangelical knowing.

A traveler was on the way, the way down from Jerusalem to Jericho, and fell among thieves who beat him, stripped him, and left him half dead. And with whom do we identify in the story? The poor, bleeding man in the ditch, for we always identify with the underdog, always take the side of the good people to whom bad things happen, because we like to think of ourselves in that way.

We've lost much blood. The sun is high in the heavens. Will we perish here in the ditch?

Down the road comes a priest. Surely a priest will help us. No. He passes by on the other side. And the crowd, always anticlerical in its sentiments, loves it. "Go get 'em Jesus! Those damn, money-grabbing TV evangelists! Get 'em Jesus!"

Down the road comes a pious layperson. You've lost much blood by this time. But alas, though he *claims* to be so religious, he passes by on the other side. "Get 'em Jesus! This is great. Those Bible-quoting fundamentalists who think they know so much. This is wonderful! What a great story!"

You strain your eyes and look down the road. There is another person coming. He will be your last hope, for you have lost much blood and the sun is hot and you are

69

becoming weaker every moment. Desperately, you look down the road, down to your last hope, and you see . . . oh, no. It's a *Samaritan*. A lousy Samaritan!

"I'm okay," we tell him, as he gets out of his Buick. "Don't bother about me. I'm okay. It's just a flesh wound. (I'd rather die than get saved by you.)"

It's a parable, a story that disrupts our expectations about saviors. The lawyer has asked Jesus, "Who is my neighbor? To whom do I have to go out and show some nice, middle-class charity in order to get myself right with God?" And Jesus responds with a story about the odd way in which God gets himself right with us. Not, To whom can I be a neighbor? But rather, Who has been a neighbor to me? We are saved by lousy Samaritans, by a neighbor we hate.

Get ready to be surprised by the one who saves you, the parable warns. Your salvation may come in ways you won't like and through people with whom you wouldn't be caught dead. He came to us, reached out to us, risked all for us, and we said, "We'd rather die than be saved by the likes of you."

Right here, in this parabolically induced gap, this is where the good news can get us, whether we are the smug, self-sufficient outsiders or the complacent, self-righteous insiders.

*   *   *

Let us preachers note: There is a movement, a relentless movement, in the history of interpretation of parables, from story of subversion to story of example. The Last Judgment becomes an occasion, not for dislocation into the gaps between God's judgments and our own, but rather for us once again to reassure ourselves that we are, just as we thought, on the right side.

The Good Samaritan becomes an example of how each of us should go out and help those less fortunate . . . and we love to hear *that* story because we enjoy thinking of ourselves as self-sufficient, autonomous, not in need of saving, but rather as the world's saviors when we toss a dime to the man in the ditch to call the highway patrol. That's the way we prefer the story to end.

"The kingdom of God is like. . . ." How many of Jesus' parables begin this way. The kingdom of God is that space, that territory, beyond the mapped, explored, charted world in which we love to dwell, a surprising land where God is sovereign. The kingdom of God is that place, that moment when God's sovereignty is made explicit, manifest, lethal to our self-constructed images of ourselves. In the words of Crossan, "Parables give God room."[10] Moralisms — myth — attempt just the opposite. Myth means to close the gaps, fill up the space with rules and suggestions for better living, something you can put on a bumper sticker, a slogan for a church bulletin board.

Jesus launched a parabolic assault upon us and our constructions of reality. His parables shattered the accepted world and offered another world. They remove our defenses and make us vulnerable to God, because it is in the gaps, in the great spaces, that God can come to us, and the kingdom of God is now.

Did not he say that we find our lives by losing them? That's why it is impossible for Christian evangelism to begin with moralisms, suggestions for shoring up our world, helping our marriages, making chaste our children. Evangelism is an invitation to die and to be born, to be baptized, to move to a new world. We evangelize by provoking mortal crisis in which false securities are unmasked and we come to see that our security is in accepting our insecurity before God.

Jesus' parables, says Crossan, "intended to shatter the structural security of the hearer's world and therein and

10. Crossan, p. 99.

thereby to render possible the kingdom of God, that act of appropriation in which God touches the human heart and consciousness is brought to final genuflection."[11]

Yet let us preachers also note that there is this movement, this relentless, degenerative movement in our biblical interpretation from parable to example story, to three-point sermon. Crossan says that one can see this movement even in Scripture itself, offering the parable of the Great Banquet (Luke 14:16-24) as an example.

"Someone gave a great dinner and invited many. . . . But they all alike began to make excuses" (vv. 16, 18). One has bought a field and hasn't seen it yet. Another has purchased oxen he has never examined. Another has a new wife. The giver of the banquet got mad and sent the servant out to drag in anybody who could be found, including the poor, the maimed, the blind, and the lame. When there was still room at the table, the servant was sent out to scour the back alleys and gutters and bring in anybody who could be had. The kingdom of God is like that, says Jesus. The kingdom of God (the church?) is a bunch of nobodies at a banquet we wouldn't be caught dead attending. End of story.

But hardly had the teller of the tale been absent from us, says Crossan, than Matthew had to add his little epilogue about the guy with no wedding garment (Matt. 22:11-14). See, boys and girls? You can get in here with God's grace, you can come singing "Just as I Am," but once you get in, then you better clean up your act, put on your Sunday clothes. Matthew has obvious problems with this crowd of ne'er-do-wells at the Lord's table.

Then Luke comes along, adding Jesus' prologue: "When you give a dinner or a banquet, you be a good little boy or girl and do not invite your friends or your brothers or your

11. Crossan, p. 101.

kinsmen or rich neighbors. . . . You invite the poor, the maimed, the lame, the blind, and you will be blessed, you'll get yours at the resurrection" (Luke 14:12-14).

According to Crossan's quest-for-the-historical-Jesus exegesis, the shock of the originating parable — the sight of all this riffraff at the King's table, God's idea of a good time on a Saturday night — has been allegorized, mythologized into something tame, predictable, careful, less extravagant, less threatening.

While I'm not sure about Crossan's claim of some historical "core" to this parable as a norm for critique of Matthew and Luke, I will grant that, even as parable moves toward myth in Scripture, the church seems intent on moving toward Rotary. Preaching, once a parabolic assault on the complacent and the fixed, degenerates into flat, three-point reiteration of the conventional and the obvious. Tireless truism delivered up as gospel. We're always moving, in the parables, or in the church, from dislocating parable to domesticated myth, from the relentlessly moving, seeking, subverting God to God as the housebroken pet of the church.

So Crossan would have us distinguish between two basic types of religion: "between mythical religion, a religion that gives one the final word about 'reality' and thereby excludes the authentic experience of mystery, and parabolic religion, a religion that continually and deliberately subverts final words about 'reality' and thereby introduces the possibility of transcendence."[12]

There is thus both in the church and in our preaching a relentless downward movement from parable to myth, the tendency of both parable and church to end up as unholy securities. So Karl Barth said that "Christians go to church to make their last stand against God," and sometimes the only way for the settled and tame baptized to be reminded of the

12. Crossan, p. 105.

scandal of the gospel is for the unbaptized (like Verleen) to report their experiences of God's intrusions.

Therein is hope. Even as there is a tendency for parables to degenerate into myth, and myth into petty moralism, there is within the parabolic teaching of Jesus a counter-tendency, an ability of parable to subvert its own domestication and to break the structures that would contain and tame it.[13] Even as the church becomes fossilized into just another helpful human organization for social betterment, just another support system for the family, the church has within it the means of its own subversion and breakout. Biblical preaching has within itself the ability to create room, in the preacher, in the church. So there can be hope.

Verleen had become, for our buttoned-down, secure, self-satisfied little church, a parabolic encounter with the staggering grace of God. Through her, God disrupted our nice little Bible study and cast us adrift on uncharted waters of divine deliverance. Baptism. Such is the beginning of evangelism, the first move in communicating in an evangelistic manner.

*   *   *

When evangelical activist Dr. Tony Campolo was to speak at our chapel, a young man appeared at my office and asked to introduce Dr. Campolo before he spoke. He told me that he would like to share something of what Dr. Campolo had meant to him.[14]

"Such as?" I asked.

"Such as when I worked for him last summer, in Philadelphia," he replied.

13. Crossan, p. 104.
14. Adapted from my contribution to *Pulpit Resource,* Aug. 1, 1993).

I asked him to tell me about it.

"I got converted my senior year of high school. I was a fresh, eager Christian so, when Dr. Campolo came to our town to speak, I went to hear him. He was great. After he spoke, he asked us to sign up for his program of inner-city ministry in Philadelphia. So I did.

"Well, in mid-June, I met about a hundred other kids in a Baptist church in Philadelphia. We had about an hour of singing before Dr. Campolo arrived. When he got to the church, we were really worked up, all enthusiastic and ready to go. Dr. Campolo then preached for about an hour, and when he finished, people were shouting, standing on the pews clapping. It was great.

"'Okay, gang, are you ready to go out there and tell 'em about Jesus?' he asked. 'Yea, let's go,' we shouted back.

"'Get on the bus!' Tony shouted. So we spilled out of the church and onto the bus. We were singing, clapping. But then we began to drive deeper into the depths of the city. We weren't in a great neighborhood when we started riding, but it got worse. Gradually we stopped singing, and everybody, all of us college kids, were just staring out the windows. We were scared.

"Then the bus pulled up before one of the worst-looking housing projects in Philadelphia. Tony jumped on the bus, opened the door, and said, 'Alright gang, get out there and tell 'em about Jesus. I'll be back at five o'clock.'

"We made our hesitant way off the bus. Stood there on the corner and had prayer, then we spread out. I walked down the sidewalk and stopped before a huge tenement house. I gulped, said a prayer, and ventured inside. There was a terrible odor. Windows were out. No lights in the hall. I walked up one flight of stairs toward the door where I heard a baby crying. I knocked on the door.

"'Who is it?' said a loud voice inside. Then the door was cracked open and a woman, a woman holding a naked baby, peered out at me. 'What you want?' she asked in a harsh, mean voice.

"I told her that I wanted to tell her about Jesus.

"With that, she swung the door open and began cursing me. She cursed me all the way down the hall, down the flight of steps, out to the sidewalk.

"I felt terrible. 'Look at me,' I said to myself. 'Some Mr. Christian I am. How in the world could somebody like me think that I could tell about Jesus?'

"I sat down on the curb and cried. Then I looked up and noticed a store on the corner, windows all boarded up, bars over the door. I went to that store, walked in, looked around. Then I remembered. The baby had no diapers. The mother was smoking. I bought a box of disposable diapers and a pack of cigarettes.

"I walked back to the tenement house, said a prayer, walked in, walked up the flight of stairs, gulped, stood before the door, and knocked.

"'Who is it?' said the voice inside. When she opened the door I slid that box of diapers and those cigarettes in. She looked at them, looked at me, and said, 'Come in.'

"I stepped into the dingy apartment.

"'Sit down,' she commanded.

"I sat down on the old sofa and began to play with the baby. I put a diaper on the baby, even though I have never put one on before. When the woman offered me a cigarette, even though I don't smoke, I smoked. I stayed there all afternoon, talking, playing with the baby, listening to the woman.

"About four o'clock, the woman looked at me and said, 'Let me ask you something. What's a nice college boy like you doing in a place like this?'

"So I told her everything I knew about Jesus. It took me about five minutes. Then she said, 'Pray for me and my baby that we can make it out of here alive.'

76

"And I prayed.

"That evening, after we were all back on the bus, Tony asked, 'Well, gang, did any of you get to tell 'em about Jesus?' And I said, 'I not only got to tell 'em about Jesus, I met Jesus. I went out to save somebody, and I ended up getting saved. I became a disciple.'"

Sometimes, in proclaiming the gospel to the unbaptized, we renew our baptism. In speaking the gospel, the gospel is spoken afresh to us. God is given room.

"Other Voices, Other Rooms"

Fifth Sunday of Easter
John 14:1-12

"Do not let your hearts be troubled. Believe in God, believe also in me. In my Father's house there are many dwelling places."

John 14:1-2a

Jesus prepares to leave his disciples. Now, beginning in John's fourteenth chapter, he bids them farewell. The disciples' questions are those of little children as parents prepare to go out for the evening. Children's questions to their departing parents are always the same: "Where are you going? When will you come back? Who is going to stay with us?"

Jesus' disciples don't ask about what's going to happen to him. They ask, What will happen to us?

"You know the way," says Jesus. "You know where I'm going."

Thomas, good old, honest Thomas, speaks for us all: "Lord, we don't know the way. What is the way?"

"*I* am the way, the truth, and the life," replies Jesus. "Nobody comes to the Father but by me."

78

"Show us the way to the Father, and we'll be satisfied," says Philip.

"How can you still say, 'Show us the Father'?" asks Jesus. "Look, *I* and the Father are one."

*   *   *

Welcome again to the Gospel of John. If you've been here before, perhaps heard the previous conversations between Jesus and Nicodemus (John 3), Jesus and Mary and Martha (John 12), Jesus and the Woman at the Well (John 4), then you know that, in this Gospel, rarely is anything played "straight." Jesus is forever talking past people, engaging in doubletalk, mystery, ambiguity. Nearly every conversation must be "unpacked."

"I'm the way," Jesus says. "You know the way; get with it."

Thanks be to God for Thomas. "Lord, we don't know the way."

At first, the passage begins straightforwardly enough. "Do not let your hearts be troubled. Believe in God, believe also in me. In my Father's house there are many dwelling places."

It's a dearly beloved, straightforward passage, heard most often at funerals. It's a rare funeral that the grieving family leaves without hearing, "Do not let your hearts be troubled. Believe in God, believe also in me. In my Father's house there are many dwelling places." Then, "I am the way, and the truth, and the life. No one comes to the Father except through me."

It's a great comfort for anxious, grieving disciples to know that there is a place for us. We, who have bet our lives on Jesus, staked our future on his way and truth, take comfort that there is a place prepared for us by him, a room, a "mansion" in the King James Version, a dwelling place. Although on this campus believers are a minority, an oddity, only a small percentage of the citizens of Durham, it is a comfort to be told that our Lord is indeed the way to the Father, and that there's room for us.

In John 10:1, Jesus says that anybody else who tries to get to the Father by climbing over the fence of the sheepfold rather than coming in through the gate is a "thief and a bandit." Here, in an equally straightforward way, he says, "No one comes to the Father except through me."

Now, I know these words in John may offend your liberal sensibilities. John is one of the most abrasively "exclusivistic" of Gospels. Tolerance is a big virtue in academic circles these days. The person who, when faced with the claims of other religions, says, "Well, we're all headed to the same place," or "When you come down to it, all religions are saying about the same thing," is a person who doesn't know much about religions. Everyday, here, I work with people from a variety of religions, and I can tell you that we are all *not* saying "the same thing," we are *not* all on the same way.

Religious tolerance is not always a sign of goodwill. Often, it can be a sign of ignorance about the claims of a given religion, a simple failure of someone to take the time to sit down and listen to what a religion says about itself, careless religious indifference, which is an offense to all religions. Worse, what we call religious "tolerance" may only be our capitulation to the dominant, secular, antireligious ideology of our culture.

During the Nazi era, for example, the so-called German Christians chided their conservative Christian colleagues in the Confessing Church in Germany for their resistance to and criticism of the neopaganism of Hitler and his minions. In response to this false faith, Confessing Christians quoted today's Scripture: "I am the way, and the truth, and the life. No one comes to the Father except through me."

So before you praise too highly the nonjudgmental, self-effacing, mushy tolerance of sweet, open-minded folk around here, just remember that such tolerance can be cowardly acquiescence to the spirit of the age, majority domination, the powers-that-be.

A couple of years ago I was asked to lead a discussion among a group of fledgling RAs (residence hall advisors, upper-class students who lead in the dormitories) on prejudice and bigotry at Duke. I asked, "Have any of you been victims of racial or ethnic prejudice here? Have you heard bigoted remarks?"

No one said anything. The group consisted of a couple of African-American students, a couple of Asian-American students, and most of the rest white students. "None of you has ever been a victim of such intolerance or prejudice?" I asked somewhat incredulously. Nothing.

"Well, maybe I have," one young woman said. She was white, blonde.

"*You* have?" I asked.

"Yes. If you mean prejudiced, bigoted remarks," she said. "You see, I'm a Southern Baptist."

"Oh, yeah, I know what you're talking about," said an African-American student. "I've had professors make those same remarks about Baptists in class. I'm a Baptist too."

So before you dismiss Jesus' tough talk about "thieves" in the "sheepfold," before you put down his one way, truth, and life, consider what it felt like for those disciples to be alone, on the bottom, asking, "What's going to become of us?"

Thus when I met with some members of Duke's Inter-Varsity Christian Fellowship and they spoke of how tough it is to be a Christian here at the university — with the immorality of Saturday night in the dorms, the urbane pseudo-sophistication of many faculty in the classroom on Monday — I was not surprised when someone reached for John 14:6 as a rock, a comforting reassurance: "I am the way, and the truth, and the life. No one comes to the Father except through me."

In fact, one sophomore was honest enough to offer this

81

explanation for why she did not attend worship here at Duke Chapel. Here, she said, things sometimes get too mushy, too fuzzy to offer much for struggling young believers at Duke. "With Catholics and Jews having offices in your basement, liberals being invited to preach political rather than biblical sermons from your pulpit, I go to Blacknall Presbyterian," she said. "After all, Jesus did say, 'I am the way, the truth, and the life. No one comes to the Father but by me.'"

And if you can't see her point, then maybe you don't know how tough it can be to be a believer in Jesus here in the modern university. We say Jesus is Lord, but where is the evidence? We say that this university was founded and funded by Christians for *religio et eruditio,* but to be a young believer here is to be under assault. To these struggling, anxious believers, Jesus would surely say, "Do not let your hearts be troubled. . . . I am the way, and the truth, and the life. No one comes to the Father except through me."

I know a man who was on the way up the corporate ladder. He found himself in a management training program in one of this country's great corporations. A vice president invited him along to an important meeting in a large city so he could see how the company did business. He saw. After the day's meetings, he was invited to the bar of the hotel to "unwind." There were women hired to be with the budding young executives. He was told that the heavy drinking, the casual sex, were all part of being "one of the boys."

He resisted. He resigned. That was six months ago. Since then, not one job has been offered to him. He has been virtually blacklisted for not being "one of the boys."

So before you condemn Jesus' "the way, the truth, and the life," think about how much that young man has offered up to Jesus. Don't demean his sacrifice for the faith with mushy liberalism. Is it not a comfort for him to know that his fidelity was not in vain, that there really is no way to the Father but this one?

And yet . . .

If Jesus is the one way, then it is no plain or obvious path. Thomas confessed he didn't know the way, and Philip admitted that, for the life of him, he couldn't see it clearly. That's what's wrong with the way that sophomore from InterVarsity used this text. In quoting "I am the way, the one way," she acts as if that settles everything, ties it all down, seals it shut. No. This is the Gospel of John, where Jesus is always ambiguous, large, thick, and never plays his cards straight. His disciples never quite get the point, and everything has to be argued, thought out, unpacked. Even his "I am the way, and the truth, and the life. No one comes to the Father except through me." You think you know exactly what he means by that. One way. Case closed. My way or no way.

Jesus did not say, "Beliefs about me are the way." Or, "Having the right opinions on my teachings is the way." He said, "*I* am the way." The way to the Father runs right through what you see of the Father in me. I am the way, I who am not always easily understandable, never simple, sometimes confusing, always moving, reaching out to those whom you don't even know in ways you can't figure out, I am the way, the truth, the life. Nobody comes to the Father but by this way, me, my way.

Unlike Hinduism, Christianity has never had a race or group of untouchables. Unlike Islam, Christianity has never been able to defend Jihad, Holy War, with its Scripture. Unlike Judaism or Islam, Christianity has never insisted that believers literally or figuratively go to Mecca or Jerusalem to be enlightened. The faith engendered by the One who is the way, the truth, and the life is large, moving, of all people, nations, and races.

It's interesting that our New Testament was written in Greek. One might have expected Hebrew. It's fascinating that we don't require people to learn Hebrew or Greek in order to be baptized. That our Scriptures, virtually from the first, were busily translated into other languages is testimonial to this faith's refusal to be bound by nation, race, or speech.

I meet Christians today who would be happier believing the Koran than the Gospel of John. I've read both. If you're a person who likes your faith tied down, definite, fundamental, explicit, fixed, stay away from the Christian Gospels — particularly John.

Jesus — you know, the one who is the one way, the truth, and the life — said elsewhere, "A sower went out to sow, and he just slung seed in every direction" (Luke 8:4-8). That's no way to sow seed, some of it on the path, some in the weeds and rocks. The sower just loves to throw seed everywhere.

John's Jesus, the one who is the one and only way, is somehow related to Matthew's Jesus who told of a farmer who had a wheat field, full of weeds. His servants asked, "Master, you want us should go pull up them weeds?" "No, let 'em grow. Dandelions look good too" (Matt. 13:24-30).

A net full of fish was pulled into the boat, mixed with sand dollars, sting rays, and crabs (Matt. 13:47). God's kingdom is like that, Jesus, Mr. One Way, said.

"I am the good shepherd," says Jesus, in the Gospel of John. "The good shepherd lays down his life for the sheep" (John 10:11). The life of a shepherd for a cheap sheep? And just after promising us a safe place in his sheepfold — we believers, disciples, those of us who have accepted him and his way — Jesus says, "I have other sheep that do not belong to this fold. I must bring them also" (10:16).

I stood by the grave of a troubled brother who had taken his own life. Never a member of a church, never got it all together in his life, never figured it out. And I quoted Mr. One Way: "I have sheep who are not of this fold, and I am going to bring them in also."

Mr. One Way is busy beating a path to those "other sheep." We don't know their names. They do not appear on our membership roll. But Jesus says that, in his way, they are his sheep, and he will have them as well. That's the way, the one way to the Father.

So if you're looking for a text to feel smug about, something with which to beat Muslims over the head, a knife to sever the saved from the damned, before you quote this, "I am the way, and the truth, and the life. No one comes to the Father but by me," before you go rubbing this "but by me" in some nonbeliever's face, you better consider the questions raised rather than answered for us by this text. The shepherd who has left the sheepfold, busily seeking the lost sheep, busy loving sheep who are not of our fold, the exuberant sower of seed, is the one way. And we with our smug, self-satisfied Jesus Club membership cards say with Thomas, "Lord, we don't know this way." We who have turned the exuberant, eager-to-tell-and-embrace Christian faith into just another way to make ourselves look better, say with Philip, "Lord, we really can't see the Father. Give us eyes to see." Our loveless, tight, me-and-Jesus mentality proves we don't know the way, we can't see the Father.

I know a preacher who has gone through great pain because his denomination is in a bitter struggle. A group in his church got together, put it to a vote, and forced him out, accusing him of preaching unbiblical sermons. He has sought other congregations, but all are closed to him.

"Do you know what is for me the most comforting passage in all of Scripture?" he asked. "We usually wait to read it until funerals. But I find it comforting now. It is when Jesus says, 'Don't let your hearts be troubled. . . . In my Father's house are many rooms, many dwelling places.'"

A comfort?

"Yes. I'm in a church who acts now as if God has a very small house, with only a few rooms, only one door. But thanks be to God, God's house, according to Jesus, has many rooms, many places to dwell. If it were not so, he would have told us."

85

4

The Invasion

Evangelism is the homiletical announcement and the
ecclesial enactment of the fact of God's invasion of our
history in Jesus and thereby God's creation of a new world.

> In those days a decree went out from Emperor Augustus
> that all the world should be registered. This was the first
> registration and was taken while Quirinius was governor
> of Syria. All went to their own towns to be registered.
> Joseph also went from the town of Nazareth in Galilee to
> Judea, to the city of David called Bethlehem, because he
> was descended from the house and family of David. He
> went to be registered with Mary, to whom he was engaged
> and who was expecting a child. While they were there,
> the time came for her to deliver her child. And she gave
> birth to her firstborn son and wrapped him in bands of
> cloth, and laid him in a manger, because there was no
> place for them in the inn. (Luke 2:1-7)

We know Emperor Augustus, the great Caesar who brought
peace to all of the world during his reign. And if we have
a special interest in classical studies, we may have heard

even of Quirinius. These men, these mighty men who commanded armies, and enacted laws, and ruled the world. But who are this Mary and Joseph inserted into history? Who is the *God* who inserts himself into history through Mary and Joseph?

A smile breaks out on the face of the church. Where are Augustus and Quirinius now? These men, these mighty men, so significant in their own day that with the stroke of a pen they could send these Jews packing across Judea to be registered, where are they now? Why did Mary and Joseph have to be registered? They had to register for the same reason that black folk in South Africa had to carry identity cards under the rule of racial apartheid. Augustus couldn't keep up with these Jews without registration. And we realize why all the world was at peace. It was a Roman enforced peace with all the world under the heel of one ruthless dictator.

Where are Augustus and Quirinius now? They are dead. By the time this story was being told by Luke they are rotting in their tombs somewhere. But that baby — wrapped in rags, lying in a manger, that baby for whom there was no room in the inn — that baby's people are dismantling the world of Augustus and Quirinius stone by stone.

So be careful not to be too impressed by what the world calls "history." Don't be taken in by what the world calls "news," for there is a good news beyond the news, outside conventional headlines.

They often tell Christians that we must "face facts." We must be realistic, face facts. But such statements continue the erroneous "fact/value" dichotomy of the modern world.[1] Positivism holds that there is some fixed, objective, discoverable, describable world that just "is" — the world of science,

---

1. See Alasdair MacIntyre, *Whose Justice? Which Rationality?* (Notre Dame: University of Notre Dame Press, 1988), p. 357.

the world of political and historical "facts." Science creates a generally agreed upon system of empirically derived knowledge, whereas art, literature, religion are much fuzzier, relegated to the realm of opinions, values.

Thomas Jefferson held that in this new country there should be no law to establish any one religion, since all religions, by their nature, said Jefferson, are mere opinions. And who would want to legislate something as unimportant as opinion?

It has been one of the great postmodernist discoveries that almost everything is opinion. Almost everything is value laden. We have no way of talking about things except through words, and words, be they the words of science or the words of art, are more conflicted than they may first appear, more narrative dependent, story based.

Science is as "religious" as religion. Scientific judgments arise from some reading of the world, a value-laden account of what is important and what is unimportant. It is amazing how we have contented ourselves with the rather, in my opinion, limited explanations of science. As Thomas S. Kuhn has demonstrated in *The Structure of Scientific Revolutions,* forward movements in science are as dependent upon leaps of the imagination as movements in art.

Of all the possible things that our technology might have invented, it is interesting that we chose to invent the computer. Did we just stumble over the computer one day in the lab? No, we got the science our mythology demanded. In a world where speed, efficiency, and the arrangement of information are more important than, say, feeding hungry people in Africa, our science will invent computers before we invent new ways of producing and distributing food.

Science, like all the rest of human knowledge, is a world constructed through words. It is not that the words of science are more factual and less value-laden than the words of religion, it is just that our mythology makes the words of science seem more real and factual than the words of faith. We live in a technological world that is so well constructed from our words that we don't even know we're living in it. We think we observe "facts" in our world and then go out and find theories that adequately explain the facts. Yet we also inherit theories and then devise the experimental means to go out and find the facts that fit the theory.

There is no neutral language of detached observation. There is no way for us to find some morally, mythically neutral ground on which to stand whereby we can dispassionately observe the facts around us and then explain those facts without prejudice. Theory precedes observation. We look out of our windows each morning and see the world we have been taught to see, noticing some aspects of our world while ignoring others.

In a seminar, my colleague Stanley Hauerwas was accosted by an exasperated student who said, "What do you want out of us? Do you expect us to go back to some pre-Copernican world where the sun revolves around the earth?"

"How do you know that the sun does not revolve around the earth?" asked Hauerwas. "If you walk outside tomorrow at dawn, you will clearly see the sun coming up in the east. At dusk, it will clearly go down in the west. Any fool can see that the sun is revolving around the earth. *And yet the amazing thing is that you don't believe that.* Despite the data rendered by your eyes, your brain, you will not say, 'Look, there goes the sun revolving around the earth.' You will say, 'See? The earth is revolving around the sun.' That's an amazing epistemological conversion. At some point in your life — when was it? — we convinced you that your eyes lied and that the sun was the center of the universe, not the earth."

I do not want a return to pre-Copernican astronomy, yet Hauerwas's example may make you wonder how many conversions you have gone through. How many times have you been converted to a worldview that makes you notice some things and ignore others? Of course, the belief that the earth rotates around the sun is a rather trivial piece of information. Few will be harmed from believing otherwise. The conviction that there is no king but Caesar is much more dangerous, leading to massive carnage and destruction in Jerusalem then or in Sarajevo or Belfast now. How many times have we been converted? What description of the world presently holds us captive?

Every observation is an interpretation, the noticing of some things and the ignoring of others. Scientists are closer to artists than they have known. Reality is not something "out there" about which we are gathering more and more information. Reality is "in here," full of value in how we describe and encounter it. Reality is comprehended, described, experienced as language. The words we use to describe what is going on *are* what is going on. All of us — scientists, poets, preachers — are busy using words to weave a web in which to live. There is no world, no facts, until somebody tells a story about it. Anything "out there" is inextricably bound to the story "in here." As Crossan puts it, "The classical mind says, that's only a story, but the modern mind says, there's only story."[2]

For instance, you and I are so conditioned to believe that there is no greater power on the earth than the government, no people more important than the (mostly) men who rule in Washington or Moscow, that we cannot imagine any solution to what ails us other than that offered through armies and bureaucracies and through those like Augustus and Quirinius who command them. We certainly are not looking for a solution from Jewish peasants like Mary and Joseph. Such knowledge will not fit nicely into our modern reduction-

2. John Dominic Crossan, *The Dark Interval* (Sonoma, CA: Polebridge Press, 1988), p. 29.

isms, will not reside in our current range of experience, so we instinctively dismiss the news as impossible simply because it is so odd.

It is of the nature of modernity arrogantly to assume that its accounts of the world are objective, freestanding fact, whereas other descriptions of the world are conditioned by myth, story, or value. Modernity believes in the existence of certain "universal values." Philosophical liberalism has a political stake in suppressing differences and particularities in the search for an allegedly common, universal conclusion.[3]

As has been shown repeatedly by various groups who have been left out of our Western intellectual conclusions, our claim of universality for our point of view is more a testimonial to who happens to be in power than to the inherent nature of reality. Those in power in universities, government agencies, and corporations have the power to force their universal conclusions on everyone else. Thus people go to universities to be taught that there really are no true intellectual differences once someone has taken the trouble rationally to understand the contingent nature of the particularities that once were regarded as differences. Western intellectual life, in its Platonically induced search for universals, tends to regard differences as only apparent. Upon hearing anyone's argument, I am forced to say, "Well, after all, we are all saying basically the same thing."

The modern thinker demands that everyone, even Christians, defend our positions on the basis of intellectual criteria that are acceptable to all rational, thinking persons, criteria like "reason" and "universality." Yet now we know that *there are no such criteria*. So when theologians like David Tracy argue that Christian theology must submit itself to "publicly

---

3. See the excellent discussion of these matters in William C. Placher, *Unapologetic Theology: A Christian Voice in a Pluralistic Conversation* (Louisville: Westminster/John Knox Press, 1989).

available explanations and arguments in its conclusions,"[4] we ask, "Publicly available to whom?" Who benefits from our "intellectual respectability"? We have been warned by theologians like Gordon Kaufman, David Tracy, and Schubert Ogden that, if we fail to adhere to these allegedly common criteria, we will suffer the worst of all possible fates. Christians will be relegated to a ghetto of the mind. We shall be pushed out of significant intellectual debate. Significant to whom and debate toward what end?

Fortunately, we now know that the allegedly universal givens of the Enlightenment — the notion of universally available reason, first principles, and foundations — are more myths than empirical facts, myths designed by a very small part of the human race with certain political consequences. Even as the Western nations set forth to colonize the world, imperialistically hoping to rid the world of those who were not as "advanced" as white Europeans, so the liberal legacy of the Enlightenment hoped to banish all ways of knowing that were not "rational" — as white Europeans defined rationality.

We now know that no truth is "self-evident," no matter what the Declaration of Independence says. Everything we know, we know because of a web of images and experiences, stories and myths. There is no point out there that is uniquely certain, universally valid, regardless of point of view. Descartes was wrong. There is no firmly established starting point for thought, some freestanding knowledge, independent of the background or coloration of a system of thought. All experience is theory laden. We see what we have been previously taught to see. Our analysis is not as empirical as we first claimed.

As Wittgenstein taught us, language conjures up a world. The world is constructed of words. In our lives, as Wittgen-

---

4. David Tracy, *Blessed Rage for Order: The New Pluralism and Theology* (New York: Seabury Press, 1975), pp. 32ff.

stein noted, we all play various "language games." These language games give order, coherence, and meaning to our world. This helps to explain why, when people sometimes say seemingly stupid things about the world, their statements are more comprehensible when we realize that within their world, within their particular language game, their statements make sense.[5]

For instance, at the beginning of the Gulf War, some Mennonites whom I knew protested the war, saying that the war was a stupid idea. Most people who heard their protest thought the Mennonites were stupid. "Face facts," they were told. Negotiations with Saddam Hussein are futile. All possible options have been tried and found wanting.

Facts? All options? The Mennonites have long had mission communities in Iraq. Persecution of these communities has been a way of life for them there. They are there because they believe that it is possible to change the world one conversion to Christ at a time, because they believe that there is a King other than Caesar, because they believe that non-violence is the way God has determined to deal with the world — indeed, nonviolence is the foundation of the world. The Mennonites are not opposed to "facts." They happen to live in a different world than George Bush, so they have different "facts." Nor are the Mennonites opposed to exploring all options. They happen to have a wider array of options available to them than those enjoyed by Colin Powell. When taken in the context of the language games of Mennonite Christians, from the point of view of their world, their statements do not seem ludicrous, because all language is only fully intelligible within the context of specific ways of living and the practices of a given social life. There is no universal

5. See my discussion of the "language game" of Christians in *Peculiar Speech: Preaching to the Baptized* (Grand Rapids: Eerdmans, 1992), pp. 1-23, 77-86.

or Archimedean point where we can stand and thereby measure other cultures from some standpoint outside of the culture. That is why to understand a culture other than one's own, say, a culture like that of Mennonite Christians, one needs to be at least to some degree "converted," initiated into the symbols and the practices of that culture.

By the way, this doesn't mean that there is no "reality" out there, that everything is nothing more than a contrived set of words with no connection to what is "out there." Rather, it is to point out that George Bush and the Mennonites appear to be talking about different truth, different reality. Christians believe there *is* truth, there definitely *is* reality. Truth has a face, a name: *Jesus.*

As I noted, one of the maddening aspects of modernity is the way modern people constantly congratulate themselves on how "universal" their values are, how "open" they are to all points of view. Most religious people find modernity anything but "open" to them.

After the Los Angeles riots following the Rodney King verdict, we had a teach-in on our campus. There was a panel, which included students, law professors, and me. During the discussion, one student, a young African-American woman, became very loud, very agitated in her speech. One of the professors said in exasperation, "I am trying to have a rational conversation with you. Would you settle down and try to be rational?"

She replied, "Whenever you people tell my people to 'be rational,' we always get screwed."

A light went on in my brain. I said, "Right! Let the record show that here is a man [the law professor] who has spent a lifetime producing the world which produced the Rodney King verdict. His world tells him that it is perfectly 'rational' for a dozen ordinary American people to come together, view a video tape in which a man is nearly beaten to death, discuss it 'rationally,' take a vote, and declare that it didn't really happen, that their eyes have lied and they did not see what they thought they saw. As someone who is in the conversion business, I say that was an amazing act of conversion and I am in awe of it."

My point is that Christians are not unique or odd in that we want to convert people to our point of view. Everyone, even law professors, is in the conversion business. Christians are not peculiar in that we want to put the make on people, convert them to see things our way, whereas the rest of the world just naturally is. No, *everybody* is in the conversion business. That is, everyone is required — in order to communicate, in order to gather a crowd, in order to think — to work conversion.

Modern people are deluded into thinking that there really is such a commodity as independent, innate "reason," universally resident in everyone. We believe this because we have been converted so well into Western, Enlightenment notions of universal rationality. The conversion wrought in us is so thorough that we believe our point of view is normal, typical of the whole world. Our "reason" seems so "reasonable" principally because our experience and point of view are so limited. We are able to believe that our point of view is universal not only because we know so little of other cultures (such as the Mennonites) but also because our point of view is officially sanctioned by the government.

*   *   *

The Christian conviction that "Jesus is Lord" evokes a different kind of rationality than that derived from the narrative of "I pledge allegiance to the flag of the United States of America and to the republic for which it stands." Christian thinking is no less "rational" than the rationality engendered by the Enlightenment. The Enlightenment has no monopoly on reason. Rather, Christian reasons evoke a different kind of rationality. Our reasons make sense, as does all reasoning, within a particular narrative tradition.

It would be hard to imagine an event like the Gulf War without such Western, Enlightenment ideas as universal rationality and common humanity to back up our military. When we have a person like Saddam Hussein whose "tribalism," "fanaticism," or "Muslim fundamentalism" render him obviously irrational, then we know we have someone who is subhuman. Therefore we are better able to kill. One could argue that, from a Christian perspective, there is no more dangerous parochialism, no bloodier tribalism, than that of the modern nation, or even groups of modern nations united in the common cause of eradicating those whom modern states label as tribal, fanatic, primitive, or unreasonable.

For my purposes here, I only want to argue that such a point of view *is* a point of view — not "reality," not universally held by everyone — and you and I had to be converted into it. Only this conversion seemed easier, more natural, simply because it was a conversion reinforced, sanctioned, blessed by the political powers-that-be in our Western, capitalist, democratic society.

Conversion is a prerequisite for any knowledge. That's one reason why conceiving of the Christian life (or possibly any other kind of life) in terms of "Stages of Faith" (James Fowler) fails to do justice to the sort of radical reorientation and long-term initiation required to think as a Christian. The very idea of life as "stages" is part of the Western idea that some sort of "forward" movement is possible in life, that we proceed from some lower form of existence to some higher form. The last stage is always the best. The vision of the independent adult standing at the very pinnacle of enlightened tolerance is congruent with the Western ideal of the tolerant self as the summit of human development. I expect that a Muslim, for instance, would find such talk suspiciously tainted with Western, Christian ideals.

"Faith" — at least "faith" with its specific colors and particular contours as rendered in our Scripture — is not a universal human attribute. "Faith development" theorists begin with the assumption that the best way for people to grow in their "faith" is by questioning tradition, standing apart from their communities, and moving deeper into themselves, and they then depict that autonomous self as the highest attainment of "faith." Such a view collides with the process described by Jesus in which we become faithful to him by "turning and becoming as a little child." Two very different "faiths" are at work here.

I have been conditioned to believe that I live a story of my own creation, a narrative of my own devising, that there is no other movement in the world than cause-effect results of my own actions, or the random workings of so-called nature or chance. The gospel is a counter-assertion that in the tug and pull of what's going on in the world, God is busy intruding into the world, surreptitiously rendering our cause-effect cosmos into creation. There are hints of transcendence, incursions, that we know not how to name, much less what to make of them. We ought to preach in such a way as to make claims of divine intrusion explicit and thereby offer evangelical reality to our listeners.

"Hints of Transcendence"

The Third Sunday of Easter
Luke 24:13-35

"Then their eyes were opened, and they recognized him; and he vanished from their sight."

Luke 24:31

A year or so ago, a friend of mine died. . . . One morning in his sixty-eighth year he simply didn't wake up. It was about as easy a way as he could possibly have done it, but it was not easy for the people he left behind because it gave us no chance to start getting used to the idea . . . or to say goodbye. . . . He died in March, and in May my wife and I were staying with his widow overnight when I had a short dream about him. I dreamed he was standing there in the dark guest room where we were asleep looking very much himself in the navy blue jersey and white slacks he often wore. I told him how much we had missed him and how glad I was to see him again. He acknowledged that somehow. Then I said, "Are you really there, Dudley." I meant was he there in fact, in truth, or was I merely dreaming he was. His answer was that he was really there. "Can you prove it?" I asked him. "Of course," he said. Then he plucked a strand of wool out of his jersey and tossed it to me. I caught it between my thumb and forefinger, and the feel of it was so palpably real that it woke me up. That's all there was to it. . . . I told the dream at breakfast the next morning, and I'd hardly finished when my wife spoke. She said that she'd seen the strand on the carpet as she was getting dressed. She was sure it hadn't been there the night before. I rushed upstairs to see for myself, and there it was — a little tangle of navy blue wool.*

Thus the writer, Frederick Buechner, describes a moment, a wistful, intrusive moment of transcendence. Now, what was that? Buechner doesn't know what to make of the moment. Coincidence? Maybe. Maybe not.

I was on my way to speak in Chattanooga. And as I clung to the seat of the little airplane for reassurance, bouncing over the Great Smoky Mountains, my mind slipped back to a breakfast that I had here at Duke ten years ago, in the spring, when I was being hired for this job. There was a student at that breakfast, a law student, who asked me the question, "What kind of minister do you plan to be at Duke?"

I remembered the question, though all I could remember of the student was his first name, Porter. And why was I thinking of that question, and that student, and that breakfast now, since I had never, as far as I know, thought of it before and it had nothing to do with matters at hand?

We landed in Chattanooga. I spoke that night to an auditorium full of people. I returned to Durham. Three days later I got a note from Chattanooga, from a lawyer who said he was in the auditorium when I spoke, but he did not get to see me

*Frederick Buechner, *The Clown in the Belfry* (New York: Harper Collins, 1992), pp. 7-8.

afterwards. He wrote to thank me for my lecture. His name was Porter. He was that long ago student whom I had remembered.

Now, what was that? Some sort of glitch in the brain? Coincidence? Maybe. *Maybe not.*

The odds against such occurrences have got to be astronomical. And yet, if we had the courage to talk about them, I expect that we would find they happen all the time. It's not interesting that such moments occur, for they certainly do; what's interesting is what we make out of them. Or refuse to make out of them.

Something about us is fearful to make too much of them. I squirm as Buechner says of his dream and the tuft of blue wool, "Maybe my friend really did come to me in my dream and the thread was his sign to me that he had. Maybe it is true that by God's grace the dead are given back their lives again and that the doctrine of the resurrection of the body is not just a doctrine" (p. 9).

Maybe. Maybe not.

Maybe these moments (and I know you've had them) are coincidence. A fluke. A quirk. Then again, maybe they are playful intrusions into our so commonsensical patterns of thought — a blue thread on the carpet, a face and a voice plucked from the past — sent by heaven to disrupt us. A peek behind the curtain of exterior reality. A whisper of providence. A hint of transcendence. A suggestion that there is more to death than mere death, more to my past and present than a trip to Chattanooga.

Maybe we shouldn't make such a fuss over such moments. Maybe they mean nothing beyond certain glitches in the electrical throbs of the brain. Or maybe they mean everything, connect us with reality so deep, so real and wonderful, that if we were to look at it face-to-face we would be incinerated by its glory. So all we get is a peek. Hints.

I would hate to see you make too much out of such moments, bet too much of your life on a blue thread or a

100

Chattanooga lawyer's note. For behind the curtain there may be only emptiness. The voice you think you hear may be the wind and nothing more.

Of course, you are betting your life on something. And such moments may be far too momentary, fragile, ambiguous for you to stake a life upon. Most of us live by what we can hold, touch, and chew, not on that which can be dismissed as mere coincidence.

*   *   *

The lives derived thereby may be flat, but at least they are unequivocal. And having bet our lives on the comfortingly unambiguous, something about us is annoyed, yes, annoyed, when the mysterious vertical intersects with the sure and certain horizontal. We are aggravated that God may be a tease.

"A coincidence can be . . . God's way of remaining anonymous, or it can be just a coincidence" (p. 11). A dream may be no more than wishful thinking, or it may be a privileged peek into the inner workings of what's really going on in the world.

Maybe God really does come out to meet us, but maybe it's always on God's terms, not ours. Maybe God flirts, loves to tease us toward a reality that we — with our facts and figures, our empiricism and suburban common sense — routinely walk past without a twitch of curiosity. As one of the students in my freshman seminar said, "Maybe modern people have so many psychological problems because psychology is the only language we have left in which to talk about ourselves." Maybe we're all like the kid who wore earphones so long, volume turned all the way up, that the heavy metal music rendered his eardrums impervious to Debussy or a whisper.

Maybe we don't see God much because we've lost the capacity to look. So messages slipped to us from the other

101

side are reflexively dismissed as "coincidence," and a divine voice is heard only as a consequence of indigestion.

Ned Arnett, chair of our chemistry department, told me that the best research chemist he ever knew was a man who got out of bed every morning, looked out his bedroom window, and said aloud, "What's going on out there today?" So maybe the trouble with contemporary chemists is that they think they already know something. They go to the lab without expectation of shock or surprise. Science dies without imagination.

I took an art history course. The professor showed us Masaccio's frescos from the Church of the Carmine in Florence. I looked, but I didn't see anything special. Then she began to talk about the paintings. She showed us the way they were put together, the relationship of the figures, the interplay between form and color. And I saw. The paintings came alive for me, imprinted my brain forever with their beauty.

Sometimes, something is there, but we can't see it. Our eyes are dulled, or our vision is unformed, uninstructed, undisciplined to look with appropriate curiosity and intelligence. What would it take to see?

If what's there is God, we shouldn't expect to see it too clearly. It couldn't be God if we couldn't explain it some other way, for God is large, thick, ambiguous if God be God.

$$*\qquad*\qquad*$$

It was Sunday, and two disciples were walking from Jerusalem to the little village of Emmaus, trying to make sense out of the horrible, confusing events of the past three days. Jesus was dead. They had seen him die.

"I wasn't that close to the cross, actually," one of them said, "but even from where I was standing, toward the back, I could see that he was dead. Finished."

It was a good campaign while it lasted, but we didn't get him elected Messiah. He's dead. It's over. Finished.

And they became aware of this stranger, walking beside them, on the way. "What were you talking about?" he asked them. "You look depressed."

"Are you the only person in Jerusalem who hasn't read the papers?" they asked.

"What's up?" he asked.

"Jesus of Nazareth, wonderful prophet, how they handed him over to death, killed him. We had hoped . . . but. . . . Some of our women came back from the cemetery with some fiction about his body not being in the tomb and some vision, angels, grief reaction, coincidence, post-traumatic stress syndrome, wishful thinking, feminine hysteria. . . ."

And beginning with Genesis, the stranger "opened the Scriptures" for them, explained it all to them.

And, true to form, the disciples understand . . . nothing. Now, why couldn't they see?

When they arrived at Emmaus, as the sun was setting, they bid the stranger to break bread with them. There, at table, the stranger took the bread, broke the bread, gave the bread, and their eyes were opened. They saw.

And they ran all the way back to Jerusalem to tell the others, who were talking about some weird news, something about "the Lord has risen indeed, and he has appeared to Simon." They told them about the moment, the breaking of the bread, the curious intersection of the eternal with the mundane, the way the stranger had teased them on the road, the way the curtain had been drawn back for a stunning glimpse at the table.

*   *   *

And some even believed. But the majority of those polled said it had to be some kind of a coincidence, something in the wine maybe. Male hysteria.

Maybe. Maybe not.

5

God So Loved

Evangelism begins in the heart of God, with God's amazing predisposition toward the world and the creatures God has created. God so loved the world that God allowed the world to kill his only Son. With such a love, emanating from such a God, evangelistic preachers ought to expect surprises, dislocations, jolts. We ought to preach as if we were opening a package that could be packed with dynamite. In fact, Augustine taught that the whole purpose of Scripture is "to build up charity toward God and neighbor."[1] Sometimes it is easier to be charitable toward God than to love the neighbor, particularly when it is made clear who the neighbors are that this God loves!

That's a hopeful word, yes. But it's also a challenging, even an exasperating word.

I was walking across the Duke campus one day with my friend Stuart Henry, professor emeritus here. It was Friday afternoon, the first day of "Octoberfest," Bacchanalia on West Campus, which is justified as a means of enabling everyone to blow off the steam that has allegedly built up because of

1. Augustine, *On Christian Doctrine* 1.36.40.

overexertion in the library. We stood there, Professor Henry and I, in front of Duke Chapel, on the steps, and surveyed the breakdown of Western civilization, the drunken brawl taking place before us, the carousing and carnality on the lawn, and Stuart said to me, "Do you know what is for me the ultimate proof of our Lord's divinity?"

"No," I said. "What is the ultimate proof of our Lord's divinity?"

"It is that verse," said Stuart, "'He looked upon the multitudes and had compassion.' Reading that, I know how utterly different Jesus was from me. I look at these multitudes and want utterly to obliterate them."

I love humanity. It's people I can't stand.

The late Terry Holmes once said that he found it a useful pastoral discipline to take a seat in any large airport and sit for some time, watching throngs of people trudge by, repeating to himself the question, "Did Jesus Christ *really* die for them?"

In the Seminary, I often ask students, "What led you into ministry?"

They sometimes say, "I like working with people."

"George, have you ever actually been in a Methodist church? I'd worry about somebody who said he liked working with them!"

People who "like working with people" often make a subtle claim on the recipients of their humanitarianism — namely, that the people be worthy of our sacrifices, that the people be nice. Alas, if one really is to "work with people," one needs more than a vague sense of humanitarianism. The people can be tedious.

Late in the afternoon, when the church was quiet and I was exhausted, I'd sit down in my office, pour God a cup of coffee, and ask, "Now, let's go over this again. Why did you think it was a good idea to build a church here on Summit Drive? Okay. But why *these* people? If *I* were calling a church, I would not have called *these* people. I'd have called a better class of people."

And then God would reply, saying something to the effect that "These are *my* people. Northside United Methodist Church is *my* idea of a good time."

Jesus was preaching one day, preaching on the kingdom of God. "The kingdom of God is like. . . . It's like a tiny mustard seed, the smallest of all seeds. But if you plant that tiny seed, water it, care for it, it will germinate and grow, and grow — and produce a weed about a foot high."

The dumbfounded disciples surely said, "Well, Jesus, that's relatively impressive, but not very. We don't like being compared to a weed."

"But it's wonderful!" continues Jesus. "Birds can come nest in the mustard plant's branches — extremely small birds."

"That's still not all that impressive. We don't like thinking of the church as a weed."

"Pity," says Jesus, "I guess God is impressed by different things than you are."

The challenge of being an evangelistic preacher is the precarious willingness to allow God to use us to assemble the church, which is often a church we would not have assembled if assembling a church were only a matter of methods of church growth rather than a matter of God's grace.

One reason why I'm for church growth is that evangelism has a way of making Christians out of those who are already in the church as we are shocked by the folk God calls to be the church. People like Verleen. That's one reason why I love the liturgical gesture, in the new baptismal services of many denominations, in which the pastor aspurges (sprinkles water toward) the congregation, saying, "Remember your baptism and be thankful." Water slung toward a congregation, recklessly, indiscriminately, effusively, is a nice reminder to the church of how each of us got here. If baptism were more careful, more neat, *we* wouldn't be here. Remember your baptism and be thankful.

*   *   *

It happened at that time that Judah went down from his
brothers and settled near a certain Adullamite whose name
was Hirah. There Judah saw the daughter of a certain
Canaanite whose name was Shua; he married her and went
in to her. She conceived and bore a son; and he named
him Er. Again she conceived and bore a son whom she
named Onan. Yet again she bore a son, and she named
him Shelah. She was in Chezib when she bore him. Judah
took a wife for Er his firstborn; her name was Tamar. But
Er, Judah's firstborn, was wicked in the sight of the LORD,
and the LORD put him to death. Then Judah said to Onan,
"Go in to your brother's wife and perform the duty of a
brother-in-law to her; raise up offspring for your brother."
But since Onan knew that the offspring would not be his,
he spilled his semen on the ground whenever he went in
to his brother's wife, so that he would not give offspring
to his brother. What he did was displeasing in the sight of
the LORD, and he put him to death also. Then Judah said
to his daughter-in-law Tamar, "Remain a widow in your
father's house until my son Shelah grows up" — for he
feared that he too would die, like his brothers. So Tamar
went to live in her father's house.

In course of time the wife of Judah, Shua's daughter,
died; when Judah's time of mourning was over, he went
up to Timnah to his sheepshearers, he and his friend
Hirah the Adullamite. When Tamar was told, "Your father-
in-law is going up to Timnah to shear his sheep," she
put off her widow's garments, put on a veil, wrapped
herself up, and sat down at the entrance to Enaim, which
is on the road to Timnah. She saw that Shelah was grown
up, yet she had not been given to him in marriage. When
Judah saw her, he thought her to be a prostitute, for she
had covered her face. He went over to her at the road

side, and said, "Come, let me come in to you," for he did not know that she was his daughter-in-law. She said, "What will you give me, that you may come in to me?" He answered, "I will send you a kid from the flock." And she said, "Only if you give me a pledge, until you send it." He said, "What pledge shall I give you?" She replied, "Your signet and your cord, and the staff that is in your hand." So he gave them to her, and went in to her, and she conceived by him. Then she got up and went away, and taking off her veil she put on the garments of her widowhood.

When Judah sent the kid by his friend the Adullamite, to recover the pledge from the woman, he could not find her. He asked the townspeople, "Where is the temple prostitute who was at Enaim by the wayside?" But they said, "No prostitute has been here." So he returned to Judah, and said, "I have not found her; moreover the townspeople said, 'No prostitute has been here.'" Judah replied, "Let her keep the things as her own, otherwise we will be laughed at; you see, I sent this kid, and you could not find her."

About three months later Judah was told, "Your daughter-in-law Tamar has played the whore; moreover she is pregnant as a result of whoredom." And Judah said, "Bring her out, and let her be burned." As she was being brought out, she sent word to her father-in-law, "It was the owner of these who made me pregnant." And she said, "Take note, please, whose these are, the signet and the cord and the staff." Then Judah acknowledged them and said, "She is more in the right than I, since I did not give her to my son Shelah." And he did not lie with her again.

When the time of her delivery came, there were twins in her womb.

Genesis 38:1-27

I have never preached on this chapter of Genesis. To my knowledge, after a search in the library, no one has ever preached on Genesis 38.

Of this text, Walter Brueggemann has said, "This peculiar chapter stands alone, without connection to its context . . . isolated, . . . most enigmatic. . . . It is not evident that it provides any significant theological resource. It is difficult to know in what context it might be of value for theological exposition. For these reasons, our treatment of it may be brief."[2] Then Brueggemann adds, "The major problem in dealing with this chapter is that even close study does not make clear its intent." To which I say, "Good, then I don't have to study it. Perfect text for a preacher."

Into the wonderfully instructive narrative of Joseph is introduced this uninstructive story of a woman named Tamar, who dupes her father-in-law Judah into having sex with her. I'm aware that many folk come to church expecting to be admonished, morally edified, ethically enlightened. What on earth are we to make of this story?

The story is about a woman. But at first it seems uninterested in her, as if she is just a casual bystander to the real story about men named Judah, his friend Hirah, and Judah's sons, with the improbable names of Er, Onan, and Shelah. Did Judah have daughters? The story isn't interested in daughters or wives. It's about men, makers of history, doers of great things, heads of families. But that's the problem — family. Judah has given a wife named Tamar to Er, his firstborn. But Er dies before Tamar conceives. The levirate marriage laws (cf. Deut. 25:5-10) say that if a married man dies without an heir, then the next male kin must marry the widow, impregnate her, and provide an heir — it being inconceivable that the widow should inherit her husband's goods.

2. Walter Brueggemann, *Interpretation: Genesis* (Atlanta: John Knox Press, 1982), pp. 307-8.

Nobody in the story lingers to mourn over Tamar's plight as a widow, alone, vulnerable. Nobody stops to consider her feelings at being shuffled around from man to man. Judah tells Onan, next in line, to go take Tamar and have children. Onan disobeys because he "knew that the offspring would not be his." Onan dies (and generations of little boys get confusing messages about the evils of "Onanism").

After two funerals, Judah says to Tamar, "Go on back to your father's house. Maybe when my third son grows up. . . . Woman, you are bad luck."

Tamar has shuttled back and forth throughout the story, through a succession of funerals, and husbands, and now she is sent home. End of story. Tragic. Dead end. Yet, if you know much about the history of women in any culture, you would have to say that it's not a particularly unusual or original story. Women were dependent, of value only as child-bearers and husband-carers, a mere backdrop for what men will or will not do. It's one of those stories. But because this is the Bible, where nearly anything can happen and often does, this story continues. Tamar becomes the lead character, and roles are about to be reversed.

Judah's wife dies, Judah the father-in-law whose sons weren't much help to Tamar. And Judah happens to go up to Timnah for the sheepshearing. After the sheep are sheared, old Judah goes out with the boys for a night on the town. (I really hate to expose fragile modern sensibilities to this, but it's in the Bible.)

Tamar takes matters in hand. She throws off her mourning clothes, dabs on "Night of Ecstasy" behind each ear, puts a veil over her face, and heads for the red-light district of Timnah.

Judah sees her, but of course doesn't recognize his ex-daughter-in-law because of the veil, and he's a sucker for "Night of Ecstasy." They haggle over a price and agree on the standard remuneration for services of this sort, one young

110

goat. But Tamar, having dealt with men in this family before, asks Judah to leave his signet ring, his belt, and his staff with her until he pays up with the goat. She takes Judah in hand and it's a done deal.

A few days later, when Judah's friend shows up with the goat looking for the perfumed harlot, he can't find her. Judah says, "Let her keep the ring, belt, and staff lest she make a fool out of me." He goes home, hoping to forget the whole incident, out his signet ring, his belt, and his staff, poorer but wiser for it.

A few months later, Judah hears the gossip that his ex-daughter-in-law is pregnant because she has been working as a prostitute. Well, Judah is utterly indignant. As an up-standing progenitor of God's holy people Israel, a potential patriarch of the church, Judah can't have his daughter-in-law, ex or not, embarrassing the family name. In a singular act of righteous indignation, Judah says, "Bring her here to be burned. It will teach her a lesson."

They bring back Tamar, who is now wearing maternity clothes rather than a black veil.

"Do you have anything to say before we make an example of you for all our womenfolk by burning you alive?" they ask.

"Just one thing," says Tamar. "The man this stuff belongs to is the father of my child." And she produces the ring (with a big *J* on it), the staff, and the belt with *J* on the buckle.

And Judah says, "Er, uh, she has taught me a lesson. Court is over. Put away the torches and the kerosene. She is within her rights rather than I." No, let's translate it more accurately: "She is more righteous than I."

Judah was expected righteously to honor the obligations of the covenant, to obey levitical law and give his sons to this woman. Through her deception, Judah has been made a righteous man, despite himself. Judah, as a man, father of the family, had all the rights. Tamar — woman, widow, unmarried, childless — had no rights. She is outside the law, without legal recourse. That ought to be the end of the story, the legal, proper, socially acceptable end, as it has been the end of the story for countless disenfranchised women down through the ages. Moral of story: all you disenfranchised, disinherited people on the bottom better obey the rules — rules, you will note, that are usually made by people on the top.

But as I said, this is the Bible, so that's not the end. The story moves on to (in Brueggemann's words) a "fresh definition of righteousness."[3] Who is guilty now? Show him the ring, the staff, the belt, it'll teach him a lesson. In this story, Tamar is (surprise) vindicated. She bears twins, Perez and Serach. The family, the holy God's blessing-to-the-world family, will be continued, but not in the respectable, middle-class way Judah intended. God's determination to have a family will not be thwarted by our affected and timid righteousness.

If there's a moral here, a point of edification for all us good church-going people, it is not the one we wanted.

The interpretive footnote in *The New International Version Study Bible* says, in a desperate and ultimately futile attempt to salvage some moralism out of this text, "The unsavory events of this chapter illustrate the danger that Israel as God's separated people faced if they remained among the Canaanites." Great, blame it on the Canaanites.

No, we really despise this story, we'd love to explain it away, because it shatters our images of how God's people are supposed to act. We want the next chapter's story, little Joseph resisting big, evil, seductive Potiphar's wife (Gen. 39). We're more comfortable with that story because we think that's the way *we* would have acted in similar circumstances. Not like Tamar. Tamar has committed those sins which good

3. Brueggemann, p. 310.

bourgeois churchpeople condemn — deception, illicit sex. Judah reacts at first as the world reacts, with indignant condemnation: "She ought to fry for this!"

It reminds you of King David and the prophet Nathan (2 Sam. 12:1-7). "The man who did this ought to hang," says David. "*Thou* art the man," says Nathan. A woman was involved there, too, as I recall. "She is more righteous than I," King David needed to say.

The story doesn't glorify Tamar or justify her action. But you do have to admire the way she takes matters (and Judah) in hand, the way she wrenches a future for herself out of the clutches of oppression masquerading as propriety. She doesn't whine about her circumstances or quietly resign herself to her situation as the perpetual victim — she goes out and wheels and deals, recklessly risking all, and thus suggests a new sort of righteousness. You've got to hand it to Tamar.

A student told me recently about his home church. He said it's a conservative, "Bible-believing" church, a church that takes stands against abortion, immorality. But when the pastor's son got his girlfriend pregnant, and then confessed it, and they married, the board of deacons met and fired the pastor. That's our righteousness.

I know somebody who is a schoolteacher, teaching in one of the most poverty-stricken areas of this country. He doesn't go to church, doesn't feel comfortable there, he says, because of his (how shall we say it?) "orientation." Recently, when he was home visiting his folks, he attended church with them. In the sermon the pastor ridiculed, lambasted, worse, made fun of those whose "orientation" does not fit that of the majority of the congregation. That's our righteousness.

But in our better, most truly *evangelical* moments, is there no part of us able to love the savvy, risky righteousness of get-the-job-done Tamar, and more importantly, love God for loving Tamar and writing her into the thirty-eighth chapter of Genesis?

Yet here is my question: Why would we bring up such an embarrassing story? A story that doesn't even mention God — except as the one who killed Tamar's first two husbands? Why would we spend a whole chapter of Genesis on this woman? Forget Tamar. Savvy, yes. Wise to the ways of the world, yes. But for all that, still a deceptive, lying harlot. Why bring her up, and on a Sunday, too?

Well, because Matthew brings her up. Matthew, the first Gospel: "An account of the genealogy of Jesus the Messiah, the son of David, the son of Abraham. Abraham was the father of Isaac, and Isaac the father of Jacob and his brothers, and Judah the father of Perez and Serach by *Tamar . . .*" (Matt. 1:1-3).

Wasn't that the reason why Joseph wanted to divorce Mary quietly, because he was a "righteous man" (Matt. 1:19) and Mary appeared to be in an embarrassingly unrighteous way with child? The angel told Joseph that God was busy working out a fresh definition of righteousness there, too. So in remembering Tamar among the list of Jesus' ancestors, Matthew has reminded us that Mary was preceded in righteous embarrassment by Tamar. God's previous intrusions caused consternation among the righteous menfolk before, and they might well do so again.

You've got to love a God who would write a person like Tamar into the story of his Son. For if Tamar could slip into the beginning of the gospel, so might *you.*

I remember my first congregation. I was scandalized by their behavior, their extramarital affairs, their often lewd shenanigans. I was outraged that a person of my vocation, preparation, and ability should be stuck out there with folk like them. I complained to one of my professors at Emory, who agreed with me that it was a scandal that a person like me should be stuck as a pastor to people like them.

"And the worst of it all," said Dr. Hunter, "is that Jesus says they get to go into the kingdom before us good ones!"

As Robert Funk has noted, "Grace always wounds from behind, at the point where man thinks he is least vulnerable."[4]

*   *   *

To be a Christian means to adopt a peculiar history in which we are forced to name ancestors whom we wish we did not know. The great-great-grandmother of Jesus was Tamar. If we hadn't had Tamar, we couldn't have had Jesus. So when Jesus called forth a new family from the waters of baptism, a new, weird family, practicing a new, risky righteousness, would not his grandmother have been proud?

4. Robert Funk, *Language, Hermeneutic, and Word of God* (New York: Harper & Row, 1966), p. 18.

"We're All Here"

Pentecost
Acts 2

In a recent book,* Christopher Lasch says that the one enduring characteristic of us Americans is our belief in progress, progress that has no goal other than progress as a goal in and of itself. Our progress is the belief that it really is possible to be over and done with our past. Most of the rest of the world knows better. We may think that we are over and done with our past, but our past is not yet done with us. Witness the recent events in what was briefly Yugoslavia. No sooner were the Communists out of power than ancient ethnic conflicts surged up as if from out of nowhere. The map was splintered into Croatia, Serbia, Bosnia. Of course, these new places did not come from nowhere. They came from the past, a past the Communists thought they had eradicated through military repression and "reeducation." No. The past came back. History is not so easily eradicated. As one commentator said of the troubles in that part of the world, "We have marched 'forward' from 1991 to 1918."

I'm a Southerner, and while there is much that we South-

---

*Christopher Lasch, *The True and Only Heaven: Progress and Its Critics* (New York: W. W. Norton Publishers, 1991).

erners don't know, one thing we know about is the pervasiveness, the persistence of history. Where I grew up, a frequent question upon meeting someone was, "Who are his people?" That is, where did he come from? Flannery O'Connor once complained that people from the North "are not from anywhere."

Not me. I knew where I was from, not only geographically, but historically. My family did not have much, but we had a past. I was from somewhere. And if you didn't believe it, all you had to do was to look at the trunk that once held my great-grandfather's Civil War uniform, the old clock my great-grandmother bought from a Connecticut pedlar. Every time our family gathered it was crowded at our table, because "family" meant not that atrophied, shrunken thing known as the "modern American family," what family has become in our day, just the people living with you under one roof. Family meant even more than the "extended family" of all the cousins and aunts and uncles who gathered at my grandmother's house for Sunday dinner. Family also meant the gathering of the dead. Two centuries of us gathered at least every Sunday to share food around my grandmother's table, but more importantly to share stories. Because when the family told stories, the dead lived, they walked among us. The dead lived among us as long as there was somebody left at that table to tell a story about how my grandfather would get so upset, every Sunday, waiting on my grandmother to get ready for church, that he would start walking to church by himself, and how my grandmother would always catch up to him before he could get to church and tell him not to be so stubborn and to get in the car with her and the children, and how he would refuse and then folks would stand at the church door laughing to see grandfather trudging along the road toward church with my grandmother arguing with him out the car window so they were always late.

One of the reasons why we modern people feel so lonely,

117

so much on our own, is that we don't tell stories about our ancestors. Our great-grandparents don't know us, and we don't know them, which means that most of us are pretty much on our own in the world. There's nobody left to tell us which path to take, or how to get over our failures, or how to put up with one another. Someone has noted that, in a technological society, there is nothing for our ancestors to teach us. We don't listen to old people because technology makes the elderly ignorant. "My five-year-old grandchild knows more about computers than I'll ever know," says the grandparent. In an agricultural or artisan society, old people had all the secrets of how to plant the seed, when to harvest, how to make a chair, or how to lay a fire. Technology gives us the impression that children know more about how to get on in the world than their parents do. No one over forty can program a VCR.

Perhaps I speak too positively of ancestors. If there is one thing worse than having no history, it's having too much history. If there is one thing worse than not being able to remember, it's not being able to forget. George Will said of the Balkans, "Here is a part of the world which has produced more history than it could consume."

In some measure, that applies to us all. We have made more history, we are owned by more ancestors, than most of us can handle. The dead, lovingly remembered in nostalgic conversations around the family table, become ghosts to haunt us in our nightmares.

Being a Southerner, one of my favorite novels is Faulkner's *Absalom, Absalom!* In the book, Quentin Compson is driven from his native Mississippi to Harvard, in a desperate attempt to rid himself of his history. But he can't. Alone in his room overlooking Harvard Yard, voices from the past come back to haunt him. Dead ancestors from a dark Mississippi patrimony stalk him. Eventually, Quentin takes his own life, and when he does, it is as if he relents, lets go, and allows his ancestors at last to have him. "You can't get away from the ghosts," says Quentin.

Can this be what the Bible means when it says that the "sins of the parents are visited upon the children" (Exod. 34:7)? Can it be that each of us is born bearing a burden of vast memory, large recollection, a past that clings to us, no matter how hard we try to forget?

In a panel discussion here at Duke after the L.A. riots, a student who could have been no older than nineteen said in anger, "You brought us here, made us your slaves, destroyed our families, our dignity, and now you are trying to destroy us."

Us? None of this had happened to her. Yet all of it happened to her. The ghosts of her ancestors are with her as much as are mine with me. And none of this had happened to us, we said; at least we act as if it were ancient history. Our history has a way of silencing the voices who cried out on African slave ships, the cries of little children in the Nazi death camps. People in the past whom we don't want to remember are rendered invisible in our collective effort at national amnesia.

But in the embers of L.A., in our troubled school systems, in our dysfunctional families, the sins of our parents, even of our great-grandparents, are visited upon the children. I am from South Carolina; I believe in original sin. Oh, we talk progress, we claim newness. Every adolescent loves to believe that he or she is totally, completely different from his or her parents. Every younger generation wants to believe that it is the first generation ever to live on the face of the earth. No. You and I are the accumulation of our history, the product of our ancestors, the stuff of our past.

"Most of what we do in psychotherapy," says a friend of mine, "is to try to keep people's pasts from killing them."

Because so much of our past is so painful, many of us long for amnesia. Rather than face our history, as psycho-

119

therapy would urge us to do, we spend much of our lives attempting to outrun our ancestors. Milan Kundera says that when the Communists took over his native Czechoslovakia, two leaders, Gottwald and Clementis, stood arm in arm on a balcony overlooking thousands of their Communist supporters. The picture was reprinted all over Czechoslovakia as a kind of icon of the new regime. But by 1952, Clementis had been discredited by his fellow Communists and hung as a traitor. Kundera says, "The propaganda section immediately airbrushed him out of history and, obviously, out of all the photographs as well. Ever since, Gottwald has stood on that balcony alone."*

How much of our painful past have we "airbrushed" out? Who among our ancestors no longer stands on the balcony with us, waving at the future, because we have no means of dealing truthfully with our past?

*   *   *

Well, it was the Day of Pentecost. For us, just two weeks after Memorial Day when we remember our dead; for Israel, the festival when Israel remembers the gift of the Law to their ancestors. There at Pentecost, "Jews from every nation under heaven" were gathered (Acts 2:5). Every nation on earth had somebody there at Pentecost. Every nation, including strange nations with strange-sounding, difficult-to-pronounce names like Persians, Cappadocians, Medes, Elamites, Mesopotamians (vv. 9-11). Now this roll call of the nations here at Pentecost is usually taken to mean that people from everywhere were there, people of every tongue and tribe. The fractured, alienated peoples of the earth, broken into so many different languages and cultures after Babel (Gen.

---

*Milan Kundera, *The Book of Laughter and Forgetting* (New York: Alfred A. Knopf, 1980), p. 3.

11:1-9), were healed when the Spirit descended at Pentecost. That's how we usually interpret this story.

But Tom Long has pointed out to me that this Pentecost assemblage is not only a diverse ethnic gathering — Medes, Persians, Elamites, Cappadocians, Frigians — but it is also *a historically impossible gathering*. Those Medes who were there that Pentecost would have had a tough time getting to Jerusalem from Mesopotamia, not just because they would have had to travel a few hundred miles, but because they would have had to travel a couple of hundred years as well. The Medes had been extinct, long gone from the face of the earth, for at least two centuries. And those Elamites are mentioned back in Ezra 2:7, but not again. The Elamites were also lost in the past. See? We have here a gathering of people not only from the north and the south but also from the living and the dead.

Tom Long says that Acts 2 is saying something like, "You should have been there with us on Pentecost. We had a huge number of visitors for the service. Some were all the way from Montana. There were people from Arizona, Michigan, not to mention a whole vanload of Assyrians, a couple of Babylonians, and a nice little Hittite couple who asked to be baptized."

This strange, playful story is Acts' way of saying that, when God's Spirit was poured out at Pentecost, it was poured not just on a few but on all. It was given not just to the people who spoke Hebrew and happened to be living in Jerusalem in the first century; it was given to people who spoke Cappadocian, given to people of every century and every place. We were all there. That day at Pentecost, it was like all of our past — the ancestors whom we lovingly remember as well as the ones we try to forget, the events out of our history we commemorate with monuments as well as the ones we try to sweep under the carpet — everything was caught up, brought back, remembered, blessed, redeemed by the Spirit.

After the Gulf War, President Bush announced, "At last we have exorcised the demon of Vietnam."

We wish. That's all we want to do with our painful past — get rid of it, wash it away, forget it. But as a child of the Vietnam era, I hope we never forget what happened and why. We need to remember, need to fix those days in our collective consciousness and learn from our past, if we can. We can never learn from our past, can never get free of our ancestors, if we fail to remember, recall. It is only in recollection and remembrance that our history can be redeemed.

That day at Pentecost, we were all there. We were given the means to remember our past, to sit at table with our ancestors. Pentecost doesn't mean that everyone has this gift. It claims that the church has been given the holy means of remembrance, to tell of the "mighty works of God" as well as the silly and sometimes even sordid acts of humanity. It means that "this promise is to you and to your children" that we are able to get together with our history, that our ancestors, even the ones we have attempted to forget (like Tamar!), to "airbrush" into our collective amnesia, that all those forgotten voices and excluded people get included, invited to the table. God's blessed, forgiving, empowering, liberating Spirit was given to us and to our parents. We were all there.

6

Speech That Draws a Crowd

On the opening day of our jurisdictional conference a few years ago, the presiding bishop informed us that the good news was that our region of the church had lost *only* sixty thousand members since our last meeting four years ago.

Suddenly, I had a vision of sixty thousand bodies, sixty thousand corpses stacked upon one another. That's how many members our church had lost in my part of the world in just four years.

I fully expected someone to say, "Gosh! Sixty thousand members is a lot to lose." No. We went right on ahead with business as usual. Death, decay, decline is not so tough once one gets used to it. We come to accept death as normal, as the way things are. The church is caught with the wrong age group, planted in the wrong neighborhood, with the wrong people, during the wrong epoch. Death by sociological determinism.

What does death look like?

In the Valley of the Shadow of Death

The hand of the LORD came upon me, and he brought me out by the spirit of the LORD and set me down in the middle of a valley; it was full of bones. He led me all around them; there were very many lying in the valley, and they were very dry. He said to me, "Mortal, can these bones live?" I answered, "O Lord GOD, you know." Then he said to me, "Prophesy to these bones, and say to them: O dry bones, hear the word of the LORD. Thus says the Lord GOD to these bones: I will cause breath to enter you, and you shall live. I will lay sinews on you, and will cause flesh to come upon you, and cover you with skin, and put breath in you, and you shall live; and you shall know that I am the LORD."

So I prophesied as I had been commanded; and as I prophesied, suddenly there was a noise, a rattling, and the bones came together, bone to its bone. I looked, and there were sinews on them, and flesh had come upon them, and skin had covered them; but there was no breath in them. Then he said to me, "Prophesy to the breath, prophesy, mortal, and say to the breath: Thus says the Lord GOD: Come from the four winds, O breath, and breathe upon these slain, that they may live." I prophesied as he commanded me, and the breath came into them, and they lived, and stood on their feet, a vast multitude.

Then he said to me, "Mortal, these bones are the whole house of Israel. They say, 'Our bones are dried up, and our hope is lost; we are cut off completely.' Therefore prophesy, and say to them, Thus says the Lord GOD: I am going to open your graves, and bring you up from your graves, O my people; and I will bring you back to the land of Israel. And you shall know that I am the LORD, when I open your graves, and bring you up from your

graves, O my people. I will put my spirit within you, and
you shall live, and I will place you on your own soil;
then you shall know that I, the LORD, have spoken and
will act," says the LORD.

Ezekiel 37:1-14

The scene in the valley of the dry bones in Ezekiel 37:1-14
is a graphic depiction of contrast — the initial, complete, utter
deadliness of the dry bones, and the subsequent, stirring
liveliness after the spirit/wind has blown over the dry bones.
Refusing to speak in palatable, vague abstraction, Ezekiel
paints a scene of total death. These bones are not merely
dead, they are "dry," totally dead. Only toward the end of
this passage does the prophet make clear that these are the
bones of exiled Israel (vv. 11-14). Israel in exile has been
dismembered, scattered to the four winds, cut off from the
land of the living.

The action is in the spirit (vv. 5, 6, 10), spirit that is here
both "breath" and "wind." The spirit brings life, for Yahweh's
spirit is Israel's breath, just as it is life in Genesis 2:7.

Christopher Seitz notes that "bones" often represent the
essence, the life, of humanity.[1] The people lament, "Our
bones are dried up" (Ezek. 37:11). The Psalmist cries, "My
bones waste away" (Ps. 31:10). Proverbs says a downcast
spirit is like dry bones (Prov. 17:22). Dry bones are utter
death. Israel is dead, utterly dead. Can these bones live?

It is clear that Ezekiel, with his vision of the drought in
the valley of the dry bones, sees the spirit as that which
constitutes Israel. All the bones come alive and recognize
God as Lord. A new community comes into being, restored
by the spirit of God, just as the breath of God brought life
in the first days of creation, and just as the redemption of

1. Christopher Seitz, "Ezekiel 37:1-14," *Interpretation,* January 1992, pp.
53-56.

Jesus in the resurrection also redeemed and reconstituted his scattered disciples.

Luke conceives of the Spirit primarily as the power behind Jesus' proclamation of the gospel (Luke 4:14-15, 18), power that subsequently continues in his disciples (12:12). And why has this Spirit instituted proclamation? In order to reconstitute Israel. In order to evoke a living "body." The Holy Spirit is not simply some personal possession, some private endowment. Rather, the Spirit is power unto the formation of community.[2]

"Can these bones live?" That is the question, the pivotal point in the text. Only God knows. If there is to be life for such utterly dead bones, then it will not be through human effort, through some act of self-improvement, some new denominational program of renewal, some new homiletical technique for speaking about Jesus. It will be because of an act of God, some stunning act of creation, not unlike that of the "wind" in Genesis 1, not unlike that of the vivification of those bones at the tomb on Easter after Friday at the Place of the Skull.

God's breath shall have the last word in matters of life and death of the body.

What does death look like? I have seen death in the individual, the gradual wasting away of flesh down to the bone, the skin hanging on arms and legs frail due to illness, the last rattling gasp for breath that is prelude to the last gasp of life.

I have seen death in the institution. It's faded Sunday school quarterlies lying about a room that hasn't been used for Sunday school in ten years. Dark hallways where children once hurried to their Sunday school classes, now dark, dusty, vacant. It's empty pews staring back at the pulpit on Easter. Grass growing in the corners of the church parking lot. The

2. See Gerhard Lohfink, *Jesus and Community,* trans. John P. Galvin (Philadelphia: Fortress Press, 1984).

frantic search for some community agency, counseling service, or other group to rent unused space for a church now preoccupied with keeping a roof over its head. It's a church meeting going on about business as usual, oblivious to the stench of sixty thousand dead bodies. That's death.

I have sat in my pastor's study on a Wednesday afternoon, surveyed my parish, and asked God, "Can these bones live?"

What does life look like?

*　　　*　　　*

"We are sending you to this old, inner-city church," said the bishop. "Some wonderful people there. But they are old, been in decline for the last twenty years. Just a handful of them left. They won't expect much ministry from you. Just go there, visit them, and do the best you can."

She gulped. Her first parish was to be like this. So be it.

In her initial meeting with her board, she could see the reality of what the bishop had described — mostly older women, a room full of white hair and pastel dresses.

"I had previously thought I had a gift for working with children," she told the board when they asked about her interests.

"Then the bishop has sent you to the wrong church," responded one of the women on the board, bluntly. "We are long past those years here."

Yet in the days that followed she noticed many children passing each afternoon outside her pastor's study window, children on their way home. They weren't the congregation's children, but they were children. "God, show me a way to minister here," she prayed.

One afternoon she was visiting with one of her parishioners, an older woman named Gladys. "Tell me about yourself," asked the young pastor.

She told a story about an earlier life, a career as a pianist in vaudeville in her youth. "I played some of the best clubs on the East Coast as well," the old lady said with pride. "Count Basie, the Dorsey Brothers, I knew 'em all."

A light went on in the young pastor's brain. "Would you play for the church . . . next Wednesday afternoon?" she asked.

"Sure, if I can get these poor old bony, arthritic hands to work," said the woman. "I'll take an extra dose of aspirin and I think I can be ready."

The pastor asked two women to make peanut butter sandwiches. On Wednesday, the four of them rolled the old piano out of the double doors of the Fellowship Hall, doors that had not been opened in a decade. Gladys sat down at the piano, out on the front porch of the Fellowship Hall, and began to play. She played a medley of hits from the thirties, then moved into a little ragtime.

By 3:30 a crowd of children had gathered. The pastor passed out the sandwiches. Gladys moved from "In the Mood" to "Jesus Loves Me." The children clamored forward. The pastor told them a story about a man named Jesus. They promised to come back next week, to bring their friends for the piano and the sandwiches, for the Bible stories and the songs.

That was a year ago. Today, nearly a hundred children crowd into that church every Wednesday afternoon. On Sundays, Sunday school classes are full, taught by a group of older women who thought that they were now too old to have anything to do with children. Those children brought their parents. Where there was once death, there is now life.

That's what life looks like.

The valley of dry bones, the "valley of the shadow of death" (Ps. 23:4) is a frightening, lonely place, particularly when it's your church. Israel in exile was as good as dead, cut off, without hope. Ezekiel says Israel was like a valley of dry bones, bones so dead they were dry. Yet the vision

128

told of a wind, a holy, mysterious, life-giving wind, which blew through the valley, re-membered those detached, dry bones, and gave life, just as God's holy breath hovered over the dark waters of creation, bringing forth life from chaos, just as God's breath was breathed into the man and woman in the garden, creating humanity out of the earth, whispering life.

Church as the Result of Easter

One of the most hopeful and perplexing promises of Jesus is that spoken by the risen Christ to his followers at the end of Matthew's Gospel: "All authority in heaven and on earth has been given to me. Go therefore and make disciples of all nations, baptizing them in the name of the Father and of the Son and of the Holy Spirit, and teaching them to obey everything that I have commanded you. And remember, I am with you always, to the end of the age" (Matt. 28:18-20).

I call it hopeful because for us preachers it is a promise that Jesus has the authority, the political clout, to do in heaven and on earth what he intends. In the light of the resurrection we can therefore "Go" to give ourselves to the vocation of preaching. Our main task is not to be entertaining, or interesting, or thoughtful in our preaching. Our task is to "make disciples of all nations, baptizing them . . . and teaching them." We go, despite all the odds against us, in the light of Easter, under the sign of the risen Christ, with the conviction that, even in our faltering speech, "I am with you always."

I call it a perplexing promise because for us preachers it is a promise that the *telos,* the end result of our preaching, that which Jesus intends to do for the world, is church. We are not to assemble an appreciative audience; we are to "make disciples." We are not to evoke a nod of listener assent; we are to move toward baptism. We are not to elucidate allegedly common human experience or to tap a person's inner feelings; we are to teach something that would not have been heard had we not preached. We go, despite all the odds against us in this subjectivist, individualist culture, with the conviction that we are accountable to a higher authority than our listeners. Every time we preach, Jesus is looking over our shoulder, having warned us, "I am with you always."

Easter resulted in church. The risen Christ returned to his followers and assembled them. The life that came from death was a thoroughly corporate affair. The "resurrection of the body" means not only our bodies but also (to push Paul's metaphor) Christ's church — a body assembled from nothing but a ragtag bunch of nobodies, a crowd convened to change the world by a risen Lord. There is no way for the world to know that it is a place of death, a people in the grip of deadly, death-dealing alliances, except by the presence of the church, a people assembled on the basis of Easter rather than on the basis of the world's conventional means of gathering a crowd.

As evangelical preachers, we ought not to be embarrassed by the miracle that summons forth the church. Easter preaching keeps rubbing our noses in the oddity of this faith, reiterating that we would not have been here, together, without an odd, intrusive act of God. One of the reasons why we have so many different biblical accounts of Easter is that Easter provoked radically transformed consciousness. One can almost feel the early witnesses straining to tell what had been seen and heard; one can sense their frustration at the pitiful limits of available language and categories of thought in which to tell what had happened among them. Perception so radically and unexpectedly offered finds few linguistic, epistemological allies in the world, nor does it find many human gatherings adequate to the task of embodying Easter. Thus is discovered the church.

Church is the predominant form the risen Christ has chosen to take in the world. Therefore the goal of our evangelistic proclamation is always baptism. We must speak in such a way as to make clear that, in the light of Easter, there is no way to survive with a risen Lord, there is no way to encounter the risen Lord, except by means that are bodily, corporate, ecclesial.[3]

Sometimes we preachers, in our earnest attempts to communicate the gospel, unintentionally delude people into thinking that the gospel entails some sort of intellectual dilemma. Our sermons are so skillful, our points so well argued, our images so evocative, that listeners get the impression that the gospel must be a great intellectual leap, a huge problem to be thought out, pondered, and solved before they can believe. We thus, quite unintentionally, dis-

---

3. The point of view I have tried to articulate here is congruent with that made by Stanley Hauerwas and me in *Resident Aliens: Life in the Christian Colony* (Nashville: Abingdon Press, 1989) and in other books and articles we have done together. A number of critics, particularly those who have vestiges of the Reformed tradition within them, have criticized our stance. Douglas F. Ottati has called this "radical communitarianism," which confuses "loyalty to God and God's commonwealth with a constricted commitment to the church" and fails to encourage participation in "civic and economic institutions" ("The Spirit of Reforming Protestantism," *The Christian Century,* December 16, 1992, p. 1165). William Stacy Johnson also criticizes my argument for being "neosectarian" and for implying that "the efficacy of God's reign stands in helpless dependence on the church's own witness" ("The Reign of God in Theological Perspective," *Interpretation,* April 1993, p. 129). For good or ill, I really do think that Easter and its immediate aftermath demonstrate the rather astounding claim that God has chosen to base the reign of God upon that rather scandalously misunderstanding and faithless crowd called the church. The alternative to the church offered by these critics appears to be the conventional mainline Protestant one: greater devotion to, and increased attempts to improve, the modern democratic state. Those who have benefited from the political status quo, those who are secure in the present power arrangements, are always threatened by the conviction that God may have an alternative plan for redeeming the world to that of liberal democracy.

tract our listeners from the main challenge of the gospel, its greatest stumbling block — namely, the church.

Historical criticism of Scripture arose over a century ago in Germany when the church's book, the Bible, was taken out of its native habitat and given to the university. Because the German university had no socially acceptable function other than support of the German state, and because at that time the university was ensnared by the only socially acceptable academic discipline, historicism, scholars began reading the Bible as if our main challenge in understanding the Bible were historical, a problem of the gap between our time and the Bible's time. What had been lost was not the premodern time of the Bible. What had been lost was the church. The Bible's concern to form a living, breathing people of God was obscured. Therefore much of the Bible appeared to be odd, out-of-date, strange.

Historical criticism of Scripture is an odd reading of Scripture, particularly in light of the Bible's own internal convictions. The Bible goes out of its way not to be "historical" in the way we define history. The Bible is such a challenge to contemporary historians simply because the Bible has concerns and purposes other than those of contemporary historians. In the light of Easter, the Bible obliterates our concepts of history. If Easter is true, as we claim it to be, then there is a sense in which we know Jesus even better than Peter knew Jesus because we have been living with him and attempting to obey him about two thousand years longer than Peter. Our problem with the gospel is not that it is old and we are new. Our problem is the warning that this Jew, this risen Christ, has threatened us with: "I am with you always."

Many have noted how contemporary American evangelicalism has likewise transformed the gospel into a personal problem. Falling backward into the morass of American subjectivism, egotism, and individualism, we render the cosmic, corporate good news into a solution to my personal problems. The result is that, when we try to speak from Scripture, our words seem odd, out of place. We are offering solutions to problems that are not biblical problems. We are offering solutions that are not biblical solutions. To contemporary Americans' sense of loneliness and meaninglessness, we offer more egotism, more subjectivism, a journey even deeper into my own selfishness. "Since *I* accepted Jesus as my *personal* savior. . . ." "Since *I* took Jesus into *my* heart. . . ." "When *I* made *my* decision for Christ. . . ." As we said earlier in this book, modernity deludes all of us into thinking that our lives are self-created, a matter of our choosing our own story. The gospel taught to us by the church is a demonstration of the truth of the story that our lives are the result of God's choice of us.

I like Robert Webber's definition of evangelism, which stresses the public, liturgical character of our calling people to Christ. Webber says that evangelism "calls a person into Christ and the church through a conversion regulated and ordered by worship. These conversion-directed services order the inner experience of repentance from sin, faith in Christ, transformation of one's life, and entrance into the Christian community."[4]

Building upon the insights offered by Hippolytus's *Apostolic Tradition,* Webber calls for an evangelism that emphasizes initiation into the community of faith by stages of inquiry, participation in the catechumenate, intense spiritual preparation, rites of initiation, and incorporation into the church. Corporate worship is central to the process, an every-Sunday reminder that we did not come here on our own, that we did not tell this story to ourselves. Sunday worship is a reminder that, if we are saved, if our lives have purpose and direction,

4. Robert Webber, *Celebrating Our Faith: Evangelism through Worship* (San Francisco: Harper & Row, 1986), p. 1.

if we have heard Jesus call our name and have come forth to follow, it is all as a corporate, ecclesial gift.

That's why the pastor sprinkles the water toward the congregation and says, "Remember your baptism and be thankful." In that act, we remember that our baptism is not our achievement, an advanced degree in spirituality. Baptism, salvation, is gift, gift of the community who told us, in Jesus' name, who we are.

The gospel call is a call to be incorporated, to be baptized, to become part of the body of Christ. Christians know of no other way to be saved than this, no other hope for the world than this ragtag group of disciples assembled after Easter who dare to live in light of the promise "I am with you always."

I began this book with the story of the church's call of Verleen to become a disciple of Jesus. Evangelistic preaching begins in the preacher's recollection that, like Verleen, all of us were strangers, aliens to the promises of God. Jesus came to recollect, to (in Ezekiel's image) "re-member" Israel, and he ended up graciously calling us Gentiles as well. Verleen's story ought to remind us that we are Gentiles who were

> without Christ, being aliens from the commonwealth of Israel, and strangers to the covenants of promise, having no hope and without God in the world. But now in Christ Jesus you who once were far off have been brought near by the blood of Christ. For . . . he has made both groups into one and has broken down the dividing wall, that is, the hostility between us . . . [that he] might reconcile both groups to God in one body through the cross. . . . So then you are no longer strangers and aliens, but you are citizens with the saints and also members of the household of God, built upon the foundation of the apostles and prophets, with Christ Jesus himself as the cornerstone. (Eph. 2:12-14, 16, 19-20)

134

I agree with Walter Brueggemann when he says that one of the urgent evangelistic tasks for us preachers is to help "forgetters become rememberers," urgently to reappropriate the core memory of the church, which has so often been neglected, trivialized, or scuttled in our misguided apologetics.[5] Amnesia appears to be a prelude to accommodation and compromise. Thus I have not been able, in this book, finally to decide whether or not we are most concerned with preaching to the baptized or with preaching to the unbaptized. Perhaps the choice is a false case of either/or. While those who have been baptized have heard the story, many live (in Brueggemann's phrase) as "functional outsiders," having lost their memory of the primal narratives of faith.[6]

How was the story told and enacted before me in such a way that I came to baptism? Who were the saints who modeled discipleship for me? When did the story of Jesus come to illumine and make sense of my story in such a way that my little life became part of the larger adventure called the gospel? These are among the questions that we evangelical preachers ought to ask ourselves. Remembering that we were once strangers to the gospel, we can be hospitable to strangers like Verleen. We can enjoy Verleen's reminding each of us that the gap between us and God has been graciously — rather, miraculously — overcome by the holy wind that blew across our dry bones, by the friend who emerged from the tomb on Easter and assembled us strangers as the church.

*　　　*　　　*

Remember your baptism and be thankful.

5. Walter Brueggemann, *Biblical Perspectives on Evangelism* (Nashville: Abingdon Press, 1993), p. 74.
6. Brueggemann, p. 90.

"Easter Fear"

Easter Sunday
Mark 16:1-8

". . . and they said nothing to anyone, for they were afraid."

Mark 16:8b

At the end of this service, last Easter, after the glorious music, the majesty of it all, throngs of people were surging forth after having sung their "Alleluias" and their "Hosannas," shaking my hand, telling me how beautiful everything was, how well I did, how great it was to be here.

And then there was this young man, surely a student, who filed through the door, shook my hand, and said only, "I don't know. I just don't know."

And as we all danced forth into the warm glow of Easter — the certainty of our faith having been renewed by the music, and the message, and the crowd, and the Chapel — as I remember, he was able only to stumble. To our assured "Christ the Lord is risen today, Alleluia!" he said, "I don't know. I just don't know."

I think that young man's name was Mark.

I know that you have come to this Easter service from

many different places, with many different points of view, with differing needs and attitudes. Some of you have come because someone asked you to be here. Others have come out of habit; you are always here on Easter. Still others have come for the music. Or you are a parent visiting a daughter or son at Duke. Or the Easter bells woke you at 6:30 A.M. so you said, "What the heck?"

But I'm not concerned with that. What I'm talking about is not how you have come to Easter, but the way you will leave Easter. There's more than one door out of this Chapel, more than one way to depart from the cemetery, more than one path from the empty tomb.

You see this in the way the Gospels speak of Easter. Matthew, Mark, and Luke all agree: it was women who dared to venture out to the cemetery on Easter Sunday. Three women. It was still dark when they made their way through cold and dark Jerusalem streets, quiet at last after a weekend orgy of violence and crucifixion. They risked much. After all, the soldiers who had crucified Jesus, who had been ordered to guard his tomb, might do the same thing to them that they had done to Jesus.

All the Gospels agree that women were the only disciples left after Good Friday. Everyone else was hiding. But even these women were disciples of a dead master. Jesus was dead.

"We weren't standing all that close," said the other disciples, "but from what we could see, yes, he was dead."

It bothered the women that the disciples, Jesus' best friends, had not even given him a decent burial. Joseph of Arimathea, a member of the same council who had condemned Jesus to death, was the only person who came forward to offer cemetery space for Jesus.

So this dark, forlorn, early morning, three women went out to the cemetery to perform one final act of devotion for their departed master — to dress his decaying body with sweet-smelling spice.

And when they got to the cemetery, that place of death, the stone before the door of the tomb had been rolled away! There was a young man sitting in the tomb. Luke says that two were there, "in dazzling clothes" (24:4). Matthew says they met an angel (28:2). Mark just calls him a "young man, dressed in a white robe" (16:5).

He gave them the news, the startling, unexpected news. "Jesus of Nazareth . . . has been raised; he is not here. . . . go, tell his disciples . . . that he is going ahead of you . . ." (Mark 16:6-7).

Matthew says that the women ran back to town with great joy and began to tell everything that they had seen and heard. The risen Christ even met them on their way back. Luke says the women ran back and excitedly told everything to the apostles (who considered the women's testimony "an idle tale" until Jesus appeared to two disciples at the village of Emmaus and then to the eleven at breakfast).

You see? Mark tells the Easter story differently, and perhaps more truthfully. Mark, believed to be the oldest of the Gospels, ends the Easter story abruptly, even awkwardly and ambiguously, particularly in comparison to the other Gospels.

The last words of Mark's Gospel are words about the women, the women who have just seen the empty tomb and heard the words, "He has been raised; he is not here . . . he is going ahead of you to Galilee."

Mark says of the women, "So they went out and fled from the tomb, for terror and amazement had seized them; and they said nothing to any one, for they were afraid" (16:8).

And then the Gospel of Mark ends.

That's a letdown! What an abrupt ending to such a spectacular story. Where did the women go? Did they ever get up the nerve to tell what they saw? What happened on Monday?

No wonder that, by the second century, helpful preachers had added a few more verses to the ending of Mark. Your

Bible at home may have twelve more verses at the end of Mark, but most of the ancient sources agree that Mark originally ended here at verse eight. "So they went out and fled from the tomb; . . . and they said nothing to any one, for they were afraid."

Mark tells of no further appearances of the risen Lord, no suppers at Emmaus, no reassuring words to the women on the road back to Jerusalem from the cemetery, no breakfasts on the beach.

There is nothing but this abrupt, stunned, stupefied, silent, fearful ending. They didn't know what to say, says Mark. Words failed. They felt fear.

It would be difficult to write an Easter hymn on the basis of Mark's Easter account. You couldn't inscribe these words over the gateway to a cemetery or carve them on a tomb. And yet, they do strike a chord. I'm betting that Mark does a better job of expressing how many of you feel about Easter than do the more elaborate, refined, assured words of Matthew, Luke, or John.

If you want the resurrection explained to you, if you want Easter done in technicolor, pounded into you in sure and certain words of earnest conviction, argued scientifically, or evoked poetically with talk of crocuses, a butterfly emerging from a cocoon, or the return of the robin in the spring, forget it. The three women have only to tell, if you can get them to tell it, of Easter fear, trembling, and silence.

They had come out to the tomb as one last show of respect for poor, dead Jesus. They had come out to put a few cosmetic touches on a now decaying, perhaps already badly smelling, dead body.

Let's all go out to the cemetery and give poor, dead Jesus a decent burial; after all, it's the least we can do. We had trouble following him closely when he was alive, but now that he's dead, it's the least we can do.

It's a bit easier to be a disciple of Jesus when he's dead,

isn't it? When he's dead, you can count on him being in one place. Throughout Mark's Gospel, there is this breathless, ceaseless account of peripatetic Jesus. "After this he went there. . . . Immediately Jesus led them to. . . . they went on to. . . . Now they came to. . . ."

With Jesus, there was no time to catch one's breath, take stock, figure things out, sit back and reflect. There was only now this, then this, here, then there.

But with him dead, decaying, lying out there at the cemetery. . . . Well, in a way, when you think about it, the Romans did us a favor, we disciples who could never quite keep up with Jesus, who always had trouble figuring out what he was up to, where he was headed next. Now we know where he is. Out at the cemetery, in a tomb, sealed shut behind a big stone.

Let's all go out to the cemetery to pay our last respects. After all, that's the way we often deal with life. We like things "nailed down," so to speak. Life, this life, may not be all that great sometimes, but we reassure ourselves that this is the only life we know. We are born, we go to school, we get a job, we get married, we grow old, we die. And though at moments we may dream of something more, something beyond the known and the empirically assured, we take comfort that at least we know what to expect, at least we have a sure and certain grasp upon what is, and that compensates for any anxiety about what might be. It all ends out at the cemetery.

And though the cemetery may not be much of a destination for our journey, there is some comfort in knowing where it all ends, how it ends.

Let's all go out to the cemetery to pay our last respects. "And entering the tomb, they saw a young man who said, 'You seek Jesus? He isn't here. He's risen. By this late in the morning, he's already out in Galilee. Go, tell the disciples that he's gone on before you.'"

But they couldn't obey the directives of the young man to go and tell, at least not immediately. The first thing they felt was fear. They were afraid. Once again, Jesus had given them the slip. They had come out to the cemetery to give him a decent burial. But Jesus would not stay nailed shut, some sweet memory. As always, he had gone on before them, out ahead of them, into the future, out of death, into life. It scared them half out of their wits.

Have we come here this morning as those women came to the tomb? Have you come to pay your respects to Jesus, Jesus who lived so long ago, Jesus who did and said some wonderful things, but now is no more? You may have come to nail down your faith, to be reassured once again that you are certain.

"Resurrection? Right! Got it all nailed down, secure and certain. No problem. Amen. Alleluia. Stand and sing the final hymn."

But that is not the way the risen Christ does business. What he offers is not always certainty but more often wonder, awe, stupefied amazement.

So Mark never got around to putting the finishing touches on his Gospel, because the whole point of the empty tomb is that the story is open-ended. Like the women at the tomb, we see something, we hear something, but nothing has been explained. We must decide. He is going on before us. He isn't in a tomb. He's out in Galilee. If we came out to the place of death wanting proof, we get no proof. What we get is life, a living Lord who is way out ahead of us.

And those well-meaning second-century preachers who added twelve reassuring verses to conclude Mark's Gospel more satisfactorily weren't all that misguided, because that's what each of us must do with Mark's story of the women at the empty tomb. We must finish the story for ourselves, in our own lives. We have been told that he is not here, that he will not stay nailed down, sealed shut, all tied up and

141

secure. He will not be held by death. So if we would follow him — if we want to be his church, *his* church — it will not be to places of deadly certainty. It must be forward, into the future, out into whatever Galilee you must go to on Monday. That's where he is, that's where he'll meet you. And that good news is more than a little scary. No wonder the last word in Mark's Gospel, and in the story of the first Easter, is fear. "They were afraid."

What are you supposed to do with such a story? That's your problem. After all, you're the one who came here looking for Jesus. But he isn't here. Just missed him. By this time of the morning, he's already in Galilee. He's gone before you.

Go! Tell!

Index of Names